RELOAD

BROWSER 2.0: THE INTERNET DESIGN PROJECT

RESEARCH AND TEXT: PATRICIA BURGOYNE (PATRICIA@CORE19.CO.UK) AND LES FABER (LES@CORE19.CO.UK)

DESIGN: STATE (MARK BRESLIN, MARK HOUGH, PHILIP O'DWYER)

PUBLISHED IN 1999 BY LAURENCE KING PUBLISHING AN IMPRINT OF CALMANN & KING LTD 71 GREAT RUSSELL STREET LONDON WC1B 3BN COPYRIGHT (C) 1999 CALMANN & KING LTD

TEL: +44 171 831 6351
FAX: +44 171 831 8356
E-MAIL: ENQUIRIES@CALMANN-KING.CO.UK
WWW.LAURENCE-KING.COM

ALL RIGHTS RESERVED. NO PART OF THIS PUBLICATION MAY BE REPRODUCED OR TRANSMITTED IN ANY FORM OR BY ANY MEANS, ELECTRONIC OR MECHANICAL, INCLUDING PHOTOCOPY, RECORDING OR ANY INFORMATION STORAGE AND RETRIEVAL SYSTEM, WITHOUT PERMISSION IN WRITING FROM THE PUBLISHER.

A CATALOGUE RECORD FOR THIS BOOK IS AVAILABLE FROM THE BRITISH LIBRARY.

ISBN 1 85669 174 6

PRINTED IN HONG KONG

A CREATIVE REVIEW BOOK

LAURENCE KING

PROJECTS

PEOPLE

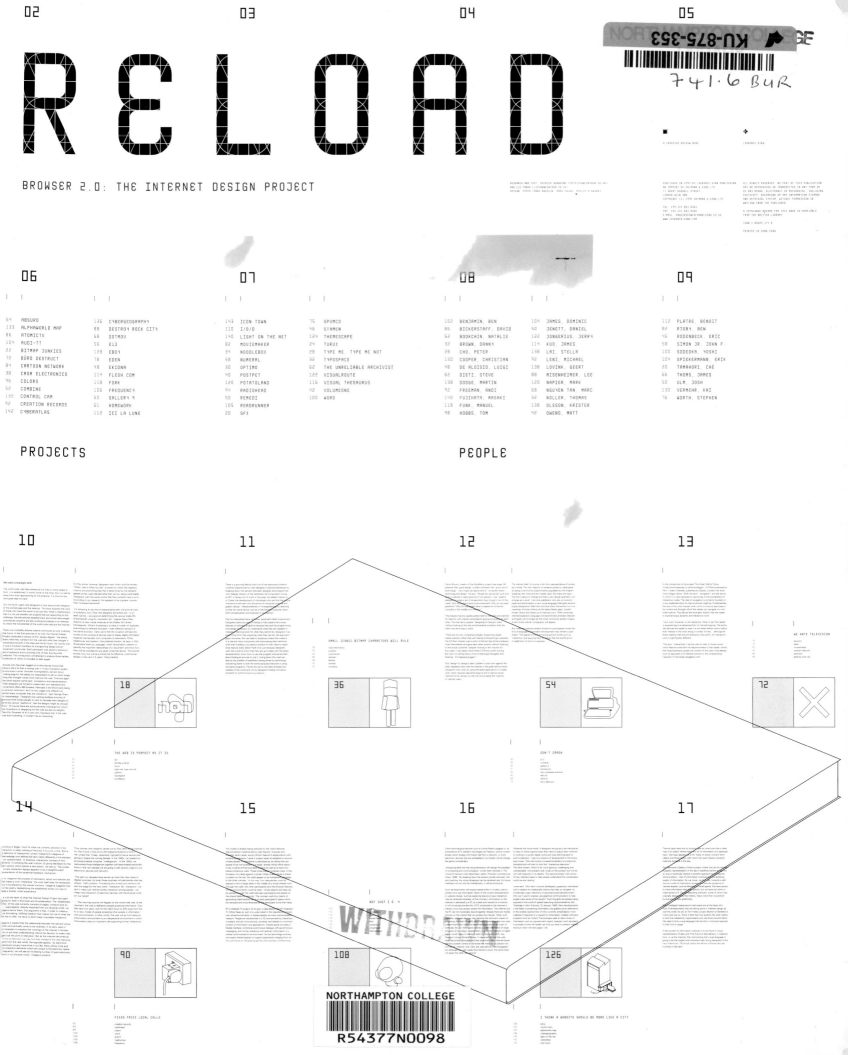

We need a paradigm shift.

THE WEB IS PERFECT AS IT IS

SMALL ICONIC BITMAP CHARACTERS WILL RULE

DON'T CRASH

WE HATE TELEVISION

18   36   54   72

NOT JUST I.E. 4

FIXED PRICE LOCAL CALLS

I THINK A WEBSITE SHOULD BE MORE LIKE A CITY

90   108   126

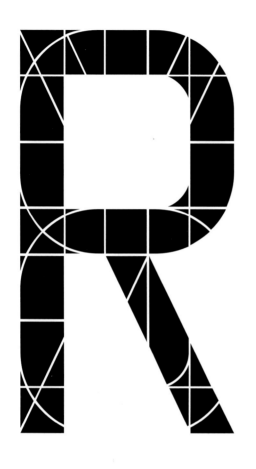 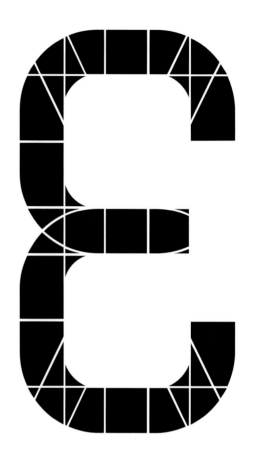

BROWSER 2.0: THE INTERNET

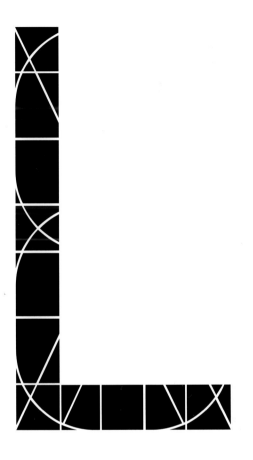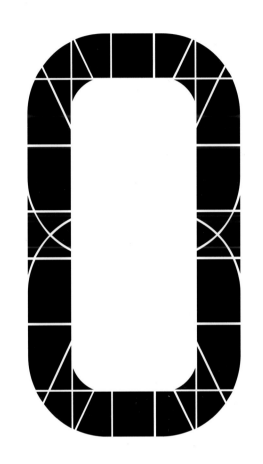

DESIGN PROJECT

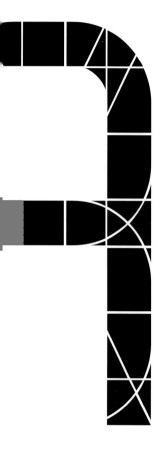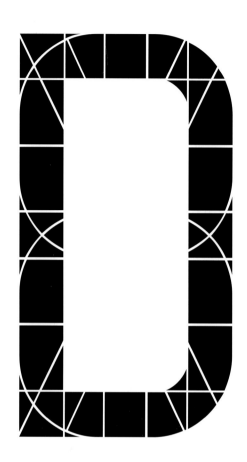

RESEARCH AND TEXT: PATRICK BURGOYNE (PATRICKB@CENTAUR.CO.UK)
AND LIZ FABER (LIZFAB@CENTAUR.CO.UK)
DESIGN: STATE (MARK BRESLIN, MARK HOUGH, PHILIP O'DWYER)

05

A CREATIVE REVIEW BOOK

LAURENCE KING

PUBLISHED IN 1999 BY LAURENCE KING PUBLISHING
AN IMPRINT OF CALMANN & KING LTD
71 GREAT RUSSELL STREET
LONDON WC1B 3BN
COPYRIGHT (C) 1999 CALMANN & KING LTD

TEL: +44 020 7 831 6351
FAX: +44 020 7 831 8356
E-MAIL: ENQUIRIES@CALMANN-KING.CO.UK
WWW.LAURENCE-KING.COM

A CATALOGUE RECORD FOR THIS BOOK IS AVAILABLE
FROM THE BRITISH LIBRARY.

ISBN 1 85669 174 8

PRINTED IN HONG KONG

06

PROJECTS

07

08

PEOPLE

09

We need a paradigm shift.

The world wide web has entered all our lives in some shape or form. It is established. It works (most of the time). But it is still far away from even approaching its full potential. It is time for the next great leap forward.

Our first book urged web designers to look beyond the metaphor of the printed page and the desktop. This book explores the work of those who have the vision to do just that. What is heartening is that it is not just esoteric art projects that are responding to this challenge; the educational establishment and some heavyweight commercial concerns are also pushing boundaries in an attempt to unlock the full potential of the world wide web and the internet.

There is an incredibly diverse creative community at work inventing the future. In the first exercise of its kind, the Internet Design Project conducted a census of this 'design digerati'. We asked them what they wanted from the web and what they thought it would become both in the near and the far future. Our survey took in over a hundred members of a burgeoning design and art movement worldwide. Each participant was asked to answer a set of questions and to provide a list of their five favourite websites. This introduction will attempt to analyse those replies, a selection of which is included on later pages.

Anyone who has ever logged on to the internet knows that there is still a lot that is wrong with it. A new frustration awaits around every corner: browser incompatibility, servers down, missing plug-ins. We asked our respondents to tell us which single thing they thought would most improve the web. Time and again, the same request came back: consistency and standardization. 'Web designers are forced to create their own standards and conventions (640 x 480 screens, Netscape 3 and Shockwave being a common minimum). As it is now, pages look different on almost every computer they are viewed on,' says George Shaw of onetendesign. 'Designers are wasting endless amounts of precious time trying (usually in vain) to translate their designs to all of the various "platforms" that the designs might be viewed from.' Of course there are some perverse individuals for whom the frustrations of designing for the web are also its delights. Take Eric Rosevear of e13.com who maintains that 'if the web was less frustrating, it wouldn't be as interesting.'

On the whole, however, designers want what could be termed 'What I See Is What You Get', a system by which the typeface, colours and everything else that is determined by the designer appear as they were intended rather than, as now, being customizable. Designers want the same control that they currently have in print. According to our research, this appears to be a greater concern than increased bandwidth.

'It's tempting to say that increased bandwidth will solve all sorts of problems, but I think that designers and artists are – or at least can be – very good at determining the various trade-offs of bandwidth, plug-ins, resolution, etc.,' argues Steve Dietz, director of new media initiatives at the Walker Art Center, Minneapolis. 'What's frustrating is to have to tweak (or duplicate) everything for different browsers – even different versions of the same browser.' Dietz warns that this situation will become worse as the universe of devices used to display digital information expands dramatically from computers to televisions, PDAs, telephones and toasters. One potential solution, he says, is XML (Extensible Mark-up Language), which should allow creators to identify the important relationships of a 'document' and know how they will be translated by any given consumer device. 'This sounds arcane now, but will be a critical tool for effective, multi-format design in the next 2–5 years,' Dietz predicts.

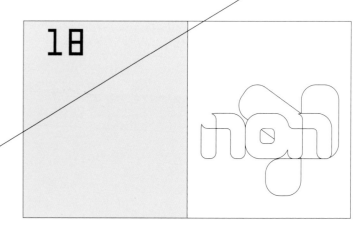

THE WEB IS PERFECT AS IT IS

There is a growing feeling that a lot of the technical problems currently experienced by web designers could be addressed by breaking down the barriers between designer and programmer. John Maeda, director of the Aesthetics & Computation Group at MIT, is doing a lot of work in this area. His stated mission is to 'foster the development of individuals who can find the natural intersection between the disciplines of computer science and graphic design'. Maeda believes in 're-engineering our teaching so that the same person can be a fully-formed computer artist – both conceptualizer and engineer in one person'.

The two disciplines have, at times, eyed each other suspiciously. Designers stand accused of failing to fully exploit the myriad features of software programs because they lack the programming knowledge necessary to understand what they are capable of. Instead of blaming tools for what they cannot do, designers may profit more from fully exploring what they can do, the argument goes. However, this can lead to situations where the creators of a site are more concerned with showcasing their technical skills than building a successful solution to their client's needs. Sites feature every latest Flash trick just because designers want the world to know that they are up to date with the latest developments, know how to use the program and are excited about finding an excuse to use it. Going down this road can lead to the problem of aesthetics being driven by technology: everything starts to look the same because everyone is using the same programs. Trends are set by the Macromedias and Adobes of the world and not by designers finding innovative solutions to communications problems.

SMALL ICONIC BITMAP CHARACTERS WILL RULE

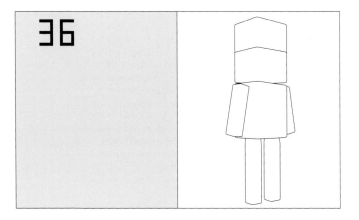

36

Danny Brown, creator of the Noodlebox project (see page 34) believes that 'good design' is often confused with 'good use of technology'. 'Let's hope we see an end to "computer fetish", technology-led design,' he says. 'People are saying that such and such a website is really good but if you asked a "real" graphic designer to judge a set of screenshots they'd laugh it out of the water. Why do buttons have to be embossed? Why do we need gradients? Why do web pages have to appear as computer consoles in the middle of a window?

'The industry has too quickly patted itself on the back and claimed its maturity with industry associations giving out awards to each other. This has led to people "designing for design's sake" without looking at the real communication problems that the client may be trying to solve.

'There are too few companies actually researching digital media solutions rather than just making embossed logo websites. The CD-Rom industry was a victim of the fact that all the producers loved themselves and gave each other awards without listening to the actual customer. Despite working in the industry for four years, I can barely name three CD-Roms worth owning. But now I'm sitting here in front of Netscape Navigator and thinking, "it's happening again".'

This 'design for design's sake' problem could work against the often repeated claim that the internet is the great democratizer. Designers who insist on using the latest applications to create work which requires specialist plug-ins and a high-powered machine to be viewed run the risk of excluding the majority of internet users.

The internet itself, of course, is far from representative of society as a whole. The vast majority of research points to cyberspace as being a community predominantly populated by the English-speaking, the white and the middle class. But there are signs that this is about to change and that a new design aesthetic will emerge as a result. 'Like zine publishers who rely on scissors, paste and photocopiers, a new visual language (that goes beyond a grey background, black text and blue links) will evolve from the machines of those without all the latest flashy apps,' predict Krister Olsson and Stella Lai of tree-axis.com. 'With continued internationalization, language will become less and less relevant as English will no longer be the most commonly spoken tongue. A new cross-cultural iconography will appear.'

But while the website remains locked in a print-based model this kind of language-independent development may remain a pipe dream. The digerati is fond of tossing around words such as 'interactive' and applying them to things that are anything but. A redefinition of terms is required.

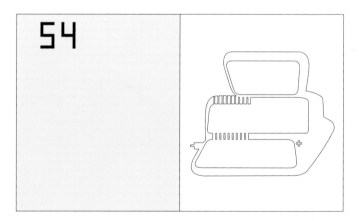

DON'T CRASH

In the introduction to his project The Great Wall of China (<http://www.easynet.co.uk/simonbiggs/>, CD-Rom produced by Film + Video Umbrella, published by Ellipsis, London) net artist Simon Biggs claims: 'Both the term "navigation" and the sense in which it is used represent a narrowing of the possibilities for interactive media. The idea of navigation is primarily founded on a very traditional notion of what an artwork might be. Fundamentally, the use of this word implies work which is more or less fixed in its content and through which the reader can navigate in a non-linear fashion. This allows the emergent illusion that the reader is experiencing a dynamic and interactive work.

'Such work, however, is not interactive. What in fact the reader is experiencing is an advanced form of channel-hopping. The author has allowed the reader to read in a non-linear fashion and to follow their interest in the work along a number of lines... although all these reading lines are pre-defined by the author. An interactive work is significantly different.

'The term "interactivity" can be used to refer to those works which feature some form of responsiveness to the reader, where that responsiveness causes the content of the work to be altered. Such an approach is in marked contrast to the unresponsive character of non-linear navigable work.'

WE HATE TELEVISION

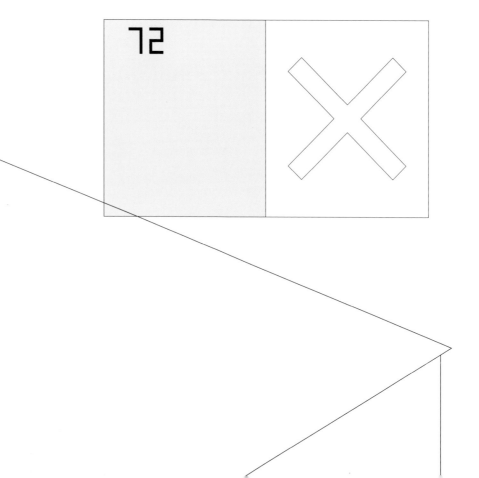

72

According to Biggs, much of what we currently perceive to be 'interactive' is really nothing of the kind. It is a con, a trick. But is his definition of interactivity correct? Masamichi Udagawa of antennadesign.com defined the term rather differently in his answers to our questionnaire. 'In essence, interactivity consists of two elements: (1) soliciting the user's action; (2) giving feed-back (to the user's action) which solicits a next action,' he told us. 'The syntax of current interaction design appears to be a straightforward representation of this essential feedback mechanism.'

So for Udagawa the process of solicitation, action and reaction are what makes a work 'interactive': the work itself does not necessarily have to be altered by the viewer's actions. Udagawa suggests that 'just like poetry, destabilizing the established syntax is a way to create a fresher, richer experience.'

This is at the heart of what the Internet Design Project has been arguing for, both in this book and its predecessor. The 'established syntax' of the web currently consists of pages, windows and so on – 'quasi-objects, directly imported from our physical world,' as Udagawa terms them. Our argument is that, in order to create a more stimulating, fulfilling medium that makes full use of what the web has to offer, we have to ditch these unsuitable metaphors.

Udagawa is hopeful that the relationship between the real and virtual worlds will eventually come to be reversed. In its early years it was necessary to express the workings of the internet in familiar terms to aid initial understanding: hence the decision to make web pages look like print or television. But as the internet becomes as common as television we may find that, instead of the web featuring objects from the real world, the opposite applies. 'As electronic experiences occupy more time in our life, there will be more and more interaction elements which are unique to the electronic space. Consequently, we will see an increasing number of quasi-electronic objects in our physical world,' Udagawa predicts.

This chimes with research carried out by Paul Saffo of the Institute for the Future (<http://www.iftf.org/sensors/sensors.html>). He writes that 'Cheap, ubiquitous, high-performance sensors are going to shape the coming decade. In the 1980s, we created our processor-based computer "intelligences". In the 1990s, we networked those intelligences together with laser-enabled bandwidth. Now in the next decade we are going to add sensory organs to our electronic devices and networks.

'The last two decades have served up more than their share of digital surprises, but even those surprises will pale beside what lies ahead,' Saffo predicts. 'Processing plus access plus sensors will set the stage for the next wave – interaction. By "interaction" we don't mean just internet-variety interaction among people – we mean the interaction of electronic devices with the physical world on our behalf.

'…The next big surprise will happen on the world wide web. At the moment, the web is defined by people accessing information. Over the next two years, look for the web's focus to shift away from this to a new model of people accessing other people in information-rich environments. In other words, the web will go from being an information environment to an interpersonal environment in which information plays an important role supporting human interactions.'

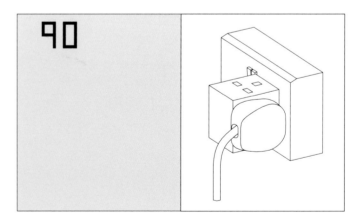

90

FIXED PRICE LOCAL CALLS

This model is already being explored by the USA's National Tele-Immersion Initiative led by web theorist, musician and scientist Jaron Lanier, and by British Telecom's experiments with immersive television. Lanier's project seeks to establish a network of telecubicles. A telecubicle is described as 'an office that can appear to be one quadrant in a larger, shared virtual office space'. It has 'a stereo-immersive desk surface as well as at least two stereo-immersive walls. These three display surfaces meet, in the formation of a desk against a corner. When a telecubicle is linked to others on the net, the walls appear to be transparent passages to the other cubicles.' In this way, four telecubicles could be aligned to form a large table in the middle of a virtual shared room. Through the walls, the other participants plus the physical features of their environments could be seen. 'Virtual objects and data can be passed through the walls between participants and placed on the shared table for viewing.' The concept works by means of generating head-tracked views of each participant's space which are sampled and re-synthesized as the participant turns their head.

BT's inhabited TV project, for its part, is described in the BT Inhabited TV White Paper as 'part of a wider belief in the importance of multi-user virtual environments, or shared spaces, as a new communications medium. People are represented in a 3D environment by characters or avatars, and can move around, converse, and interact in a common context of information and applications. Shared space provides a flexible interface, combining synchronous dialogue with asynchronous messaging, and human presence with abstract information in a unified communications environment. As the technology evolves, we expect shared spaces to support applications ranging from on-line commerce to role-playing games and business conferencing.'

NOT JUST I.E. 4

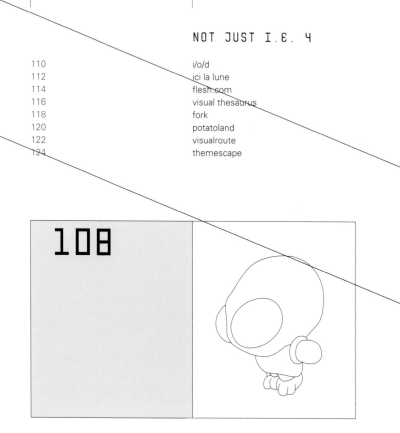

108

Other technological devices such as Virtual Reality goggles or, as predicted by BT's resident futurologist Ian Pearson, active contact lenses which display information fed from a network, or even electronic devices that are embedded in our bodies will all change the game considerably.

'Introducing flesh into the virtual dimension will change the paradigm of computing and communication,' wrote Stahl Stenslie in *The Virtual Dimension* (John Beckmann, editor, Princeton Architectural Press, 1998). 'By breaking down the sensory border between man and machine, the virtual dimension can be rendered real. Its future interface will not only be multisensory, it will be emotional.'

Such developments will require radical shifts in models used to present and use information. Much of the current developments in website design, such as exploring television-type metaphors may be rendered obsolete. At the moment, information on the internet is delivered to a PC on a desk and viewed on a monitor. It will not always be like this. A PC connected to the internet is merely a two-way access system for information. The internet and the PC are not inextricably bound together. Already there are mobile phones on the market that can access the internet. Other such portable, personal devices may become the dominant means of accessing the web if it shifts from being something that one uses predominantly for work and becomes more and more a part of everyday life. An information delivery system that relies on large amounts of text-heavy, layered links, like so many sheets of digital paper would make no sense if used in conjunction with, say, Pearson's active contact lenses. It may even be that the web itself becomes outmoded and that an entirely new internet-based delivery system comes to dominate the medium: at present the two terms 'internet' and 'web' are used almost interchangeably but although the web needs the internet to exist, the same does not apply the other way around.

Whatever the future holds, if designers are going to be well-placed to react to online opportunities they need to adjust their mind-set to working in a purely digital world and stop referring back to print or television. 'I see two streams of development in the future,' says Lanier. 'One will involve increased emphasis on production standards and will start to look like "interactive television". The other stream, which is far more glorious, challenging and unpredictable, will probably look crude on the surface, but will be rich with treasures in its depths. This second stream will consist of new interface ideas to help people understand the complicated world we are creating.'

Lanier asks: 'Why hasn't anyone developed a graphical, web-based tool to replace the inadequate menus that help us navigate our increasingly huge collections of personal bookmarks/favorites? Why can't search engines use graphical communication to help people make sense of the results?' Such thoughts are already being explored in the world of spatial searching (documented by Nat Tunbridge in *New Scientist*, 23 January 1999). New developments in the fields of presenting information use graphics as an alternative to the endless layered lists of links currently employed by most websites in response to a request for information. Instead, software programs such as Cartia's ThemeScape seek to take a body of information such as a government report, analyse it and represent it pictorially so that the reader can find out what it contains without having to read it all (see page 124).

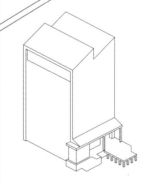

I THINK A WEBSITE SHOULD BE MORE LIKE A CITY

ThemeScape does this by plotting data as what looks like a relief map of an island. Where there is a lot of information on a particular topic, that topic appears as a hill. Areas of lesser concern form valleys and those topics with which the report barely concerns itself are dumped in the sea.

Earl Rennison's Galaxy of News project where one can fly through a graphic representation of the day's headlines before diving into an area of particular interest is another approach to solving the same problem – that of information overload and the declining quality of information. As we move, via the web, towards a self-service model of information access, we lose the guidance of 'domain experts' such as librarians or travel agents. We have access to more information than ever before, but we have less time to make sense of it. Spatial searching software, some of which was originally designed by the military, helps solve that conundrum by expressing data graphically.

Such intelligent responses to real needs are at the heart of a host of developments that are taking place in website design all over the world. As yet, as Tom Hobbs, project director on Benetton's Colors site told us, 'there is little that truly exploits the web's ability to host true interactivity, hyper-linearity and user-driven environments. We need to find a visual language that has this in mind and responds to that kind of usage.'

If the solution to information overload is to be found in visual representations of data, and if the future of data delivery, in whatever form, is via the internet, then discovering that visual language is going to be the single most important task facing designers in the new millennium. This book charts the efforts of those who are involved in that task.

18

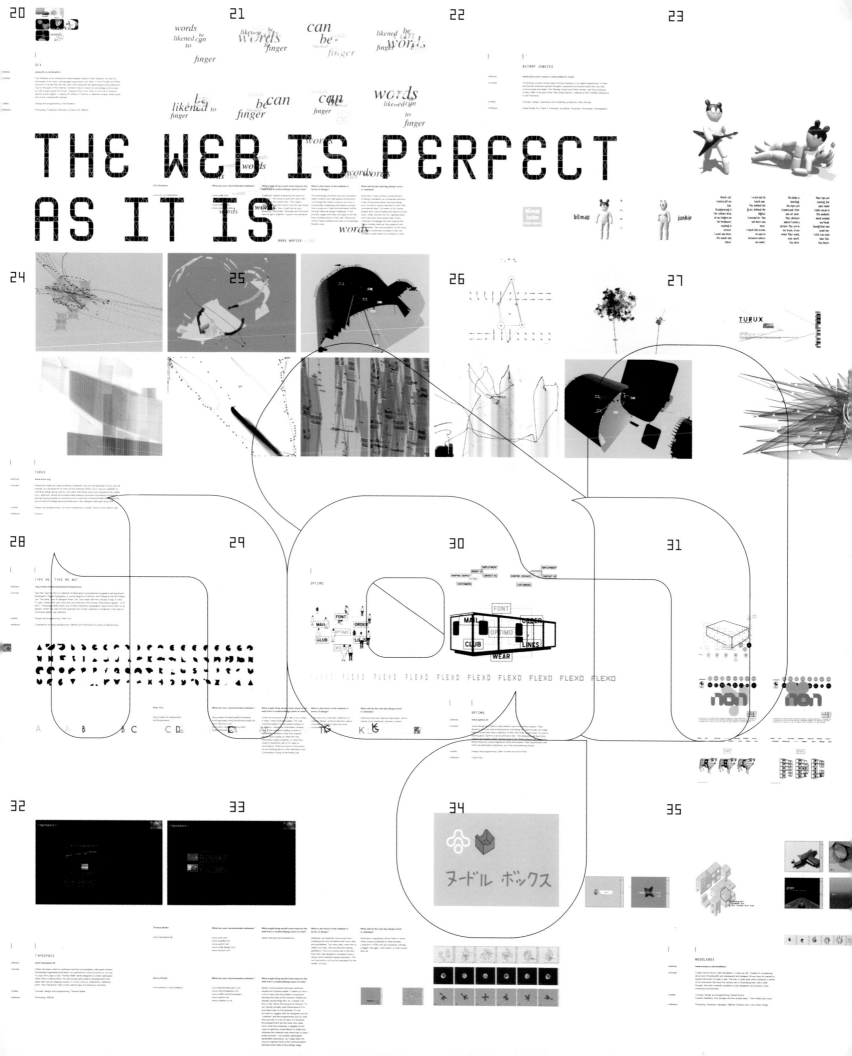

word

likened

to

SFX

address | www.sfx.co.nz/tamahori

concept

Ché Tamahori is an interactive media designer based in New Zealand. His site is a showcase of his work, cutting-edge experiments and ideas. In the Thought and Place sections of the site the user may view work using the very latest plug-ins and extensions. True to the spirit of the internet, Tamahori likes to share his knowledge and he does so with a keen sense of humour. Typical of this is his 'How To Cook 3D In Director' section which begins: 'Creating 3D effects in Director is relatively simple, tastes great and is low in bandwidth calories.'

credits

Design and programming: Ché Tamahori

software

Photoshop, Freehand, Premiere, Extreme 3D, BBEdit

liken

finger

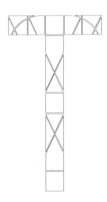
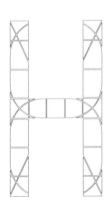
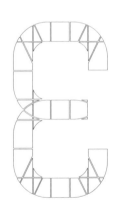
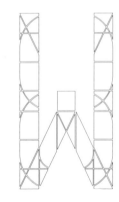

Ché Tamahori

↖ www.sfx.co.nz/tamahori

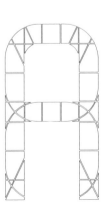
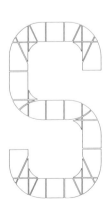
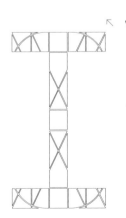
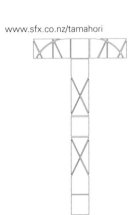

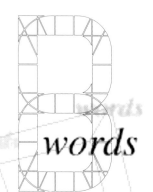
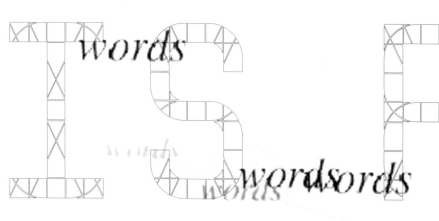

likened be
words a
small big
to finger

ger

can
be words a
likened to
finger

likened be
can a
finger words

fade to

words
be can a
likened finger to

words
can be a
finger likened

words
likened can
to fing

CRISP

words
words
words
words
words words
words
words
words

What are your recommended websites?

www.useit.com
www.lessrain.com
www.volumeone.com
www.hotbot.com
www.wired.com/news

What single thing would most improve the web from a creative/design point of view?

Creatively: people embracing the nature of the web – not trying to push print and video aesthetics into online form. This means relinquishing some control over the way things look on screen; this in itself can be very liberating. Technically: Netscape and Microsoft have to get it together. Support the standards.

What is the future of the website in terms of design?

The technology will drive the new revolution; cable modems and high-speed connections *will* change the online world as we know it. Dynamically integrating information sources that include text, video and animation will be the big millennial design challenge. In the process, pages and sites will cease to be the basic building blocks of the web. Resources will be made available and used in increasingly flexible ways.

What will be the next big design trend in websites?

Short-term, there will be a retrenchment of design standards, as companies become more conservative about the technology and connection speed required to view their commercial sites. For better or for worse, people aren't downloading the latest browser every week, and the net isn't getting faster. We'll see even more portal sites. Every corporate homepage will start looking like Yahoo: simple mark-up, few graphics and a jillion links. The one exception to this trend could be a continued increase in the use of Flash to add sizzle (not content) to sites.

BITMAP JUNKIES

address	www.sirius.com/~maxk or www.xs4all.nl/~maxk
concept	The Bitmap Junkies stories seek to bring meaning to our digital experiences. A male and female character express thoughts, questions and doubts about the way they communicate and relate. The 'Bitmap Junkie and Other Stories' was first produced in May 1998, to be part of the 'New Body Electric' website of the FUSE98 conference in San Francisco.
credits	Concept, design, characters and modelling, production: Max Kisman
software	Strata Studio Pro, Flash 3, Premiere, SoundEdit, Illustrator, Photoshop, Fontographer

er

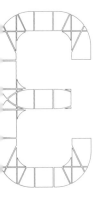
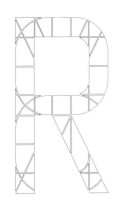
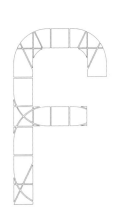
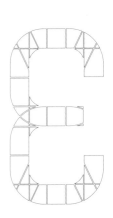
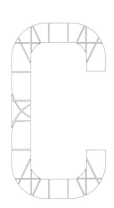
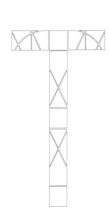

bitmap junkie & other stories

bitmap

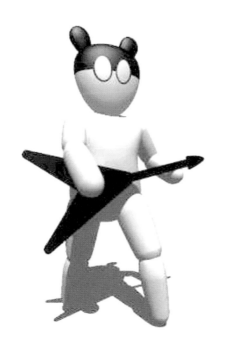

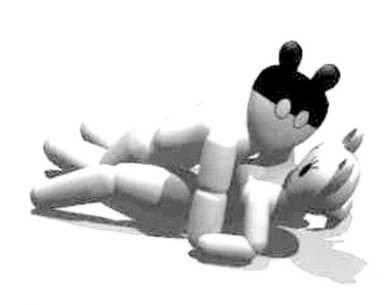

junkie

Words roll slowly off my lips. Disappearing in the rythmic beat of my fingers on the keyboard, reading in silence. I want you here. My words you there.

I reach out to touch you. You behind the glass, behind the digital transporter. You not here you here. I touch the screen on you in between where we meet.

My body is bending. My eyes are closed and I feel you all over. Your absence doesn't need a picture. You are in my brain, in my veins. Your mind, your spirit. You here.

Your lips are moving, but your voice fades away in the ambient noise around my head. Saying that you want me. I still can read your lips. You there.

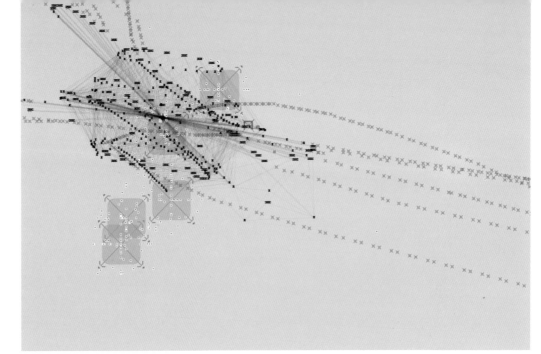

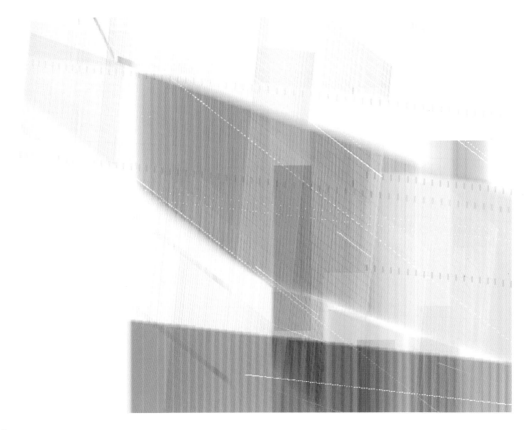

TURUX

address	www.turux.org
concept	Interactive media are rarely soothing or beautiful, but just one glimpse of turux.org will change your perceptions of what can be achieved online. Turux was put together by Viennese design group Dextro, who claim that these works are inspired by the 'highly toxic, addictive, severe-drowsiness-hallucinations-confusion-convulsions-combative-and-self-injurious-behavior-respiratory-arrest-seizures-coma-and-finally-death-inducing, soon-to-become-illegal grievous-bodily-harm new designer date-rape drug GHB'.
credits	Design and programming: Lia (www.silverserver.co.at/lia), Dextro (www.dextro.org)
software	Director

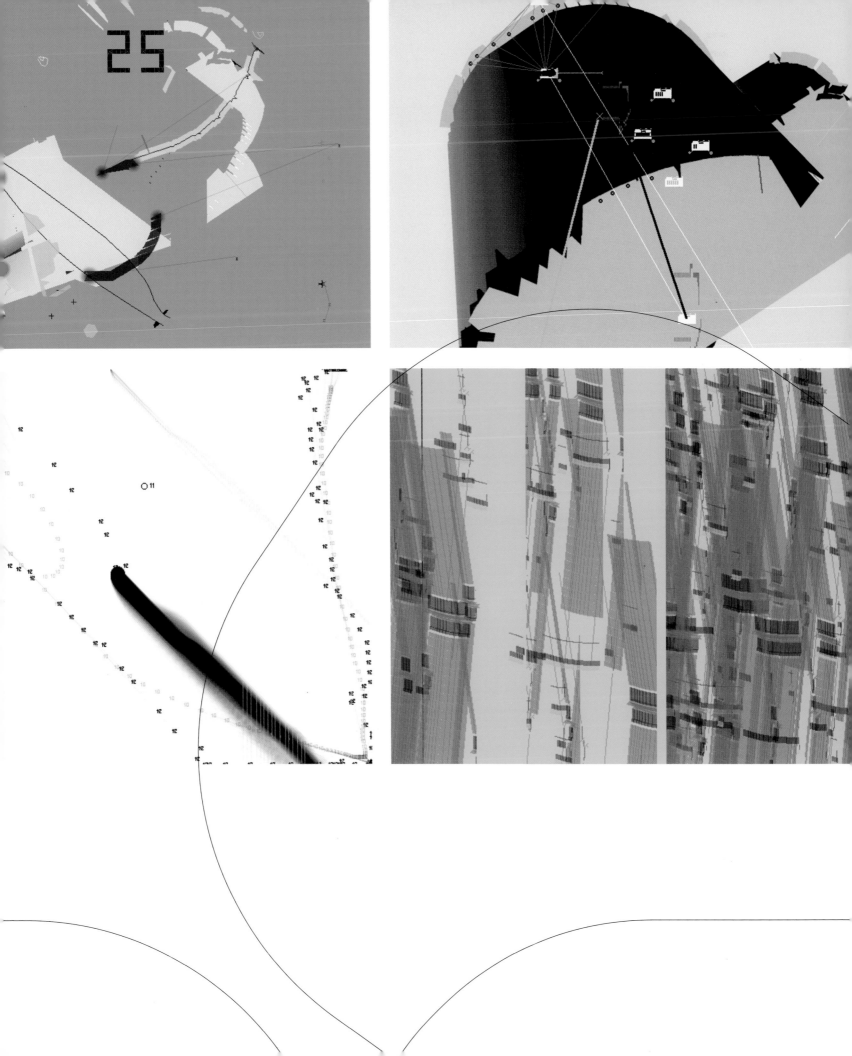

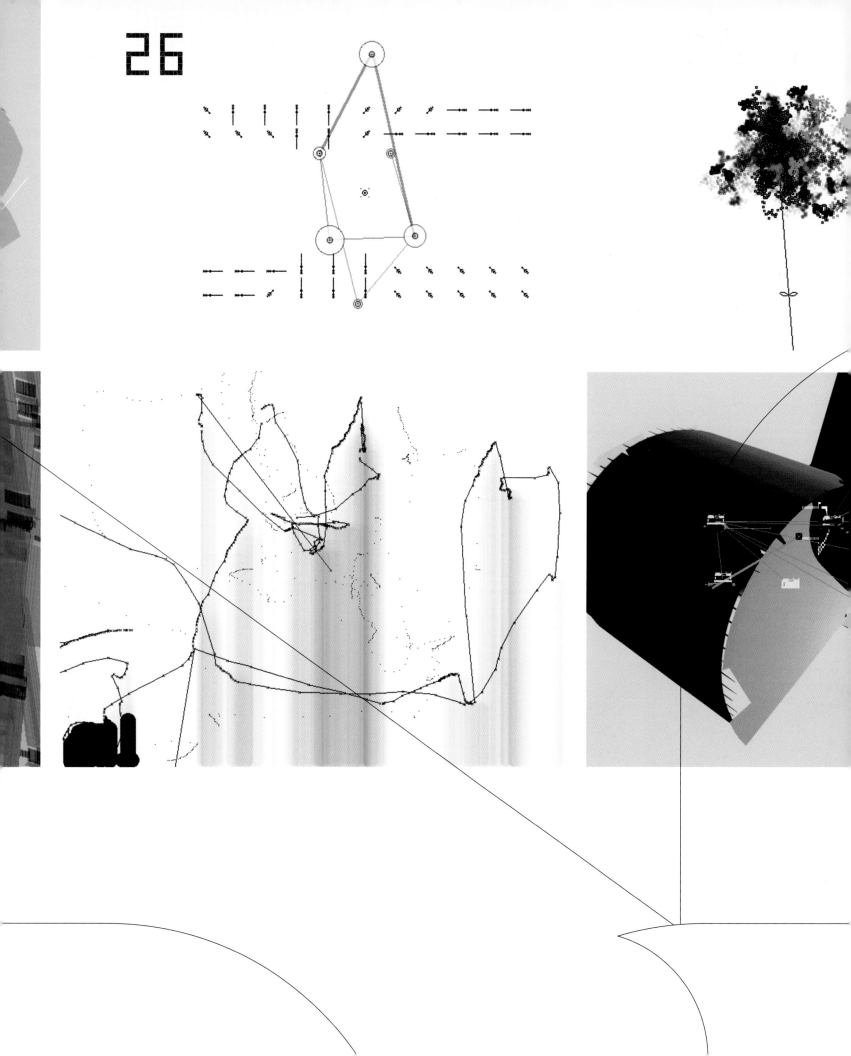

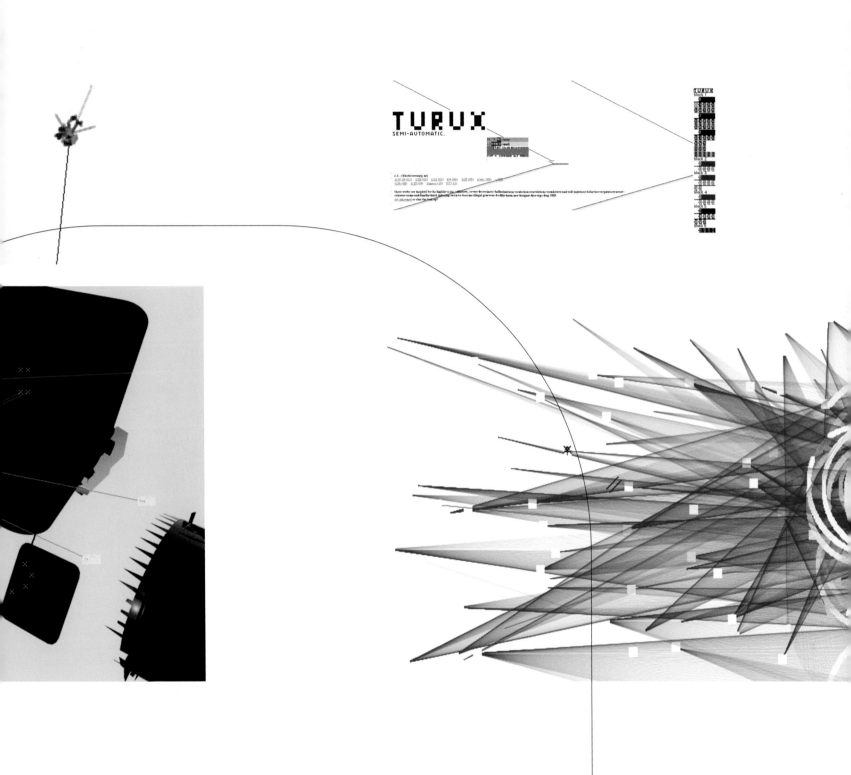

TURUX
SEMI-AUTOMATIC.

TYPE ME, TYPE ME NOT

address	//acg.media.mit.edu/people/pcho/typemenot
concept	Type Me, Type Me Not is a collection of ideas about computational typography and expression, developed in Digital Typography, a course taught by Professor John Maeda at the MIT Media Lab. The piece, says its designer Peter Cho, was made with the concept of play in mind. To 'play' a letter, the user must click and hold down the mouse; three letters appear – A, B and C. Choosing a letter starts one of three interactive typographic experiments that run as applets. When the user hits the keyboard the chosen character is rendered in the style of whichever applet was selected.
credits	Design and programming: Peter Cho
software	CodeWarrior for Java development. BBEdit and Photoshop for some incidental tasks.

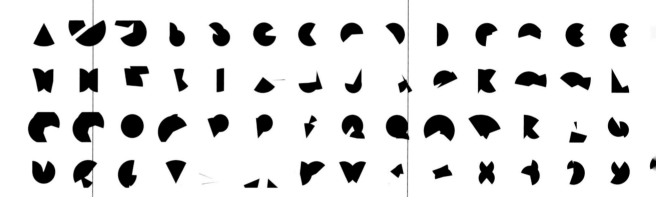

Peter Cho

↖ //acg.media.mit.edu/people/
pcho/typemenot

OPTIMO

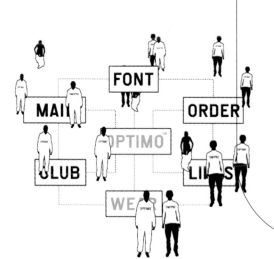

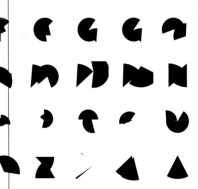

What are your recommended websites?

//acg.media.mit.edu/mas961/exhibition
www.geocities.com/SoHo/Workshop/8184
www.theonion.com
www.astro.virginia.edu/~eww6n/
TreasureTroves.html

What single thing would most improve the web from a creative/design point of view?

I think the structure of the web is too rooted in static, interconnected pages. The web would be better if it was based instead on a dynamic, interactive information stream. One of the problems holding us back is bandwidth. Another is that few creative people have a grasp on what the new information space could be, or what they could or should do with it if it were to come about. These are some of the issues we are thinking about in the Aesthetics and Computation Group at the Media Lab.

What is the future of the website in terms of design?

I see more of a cinematic influence on website design, as the production values of broadcast graphics become more common online.

What will be the next big design trend in websites?

Flash and Java are making a big impact. We're seeing more streamed, dynamic content.

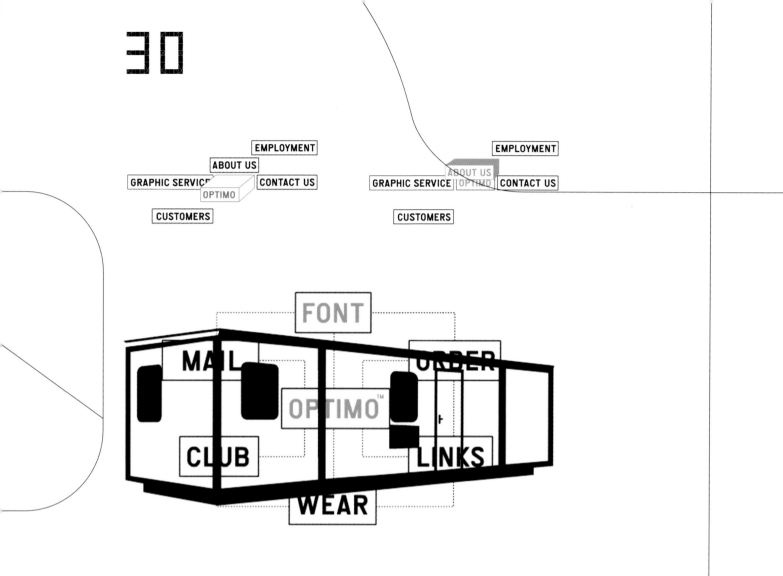

EMPLOYMENT
ABOUT US
GRAPHIC SERVICE   CONTACT US
OPTIMO
CUSTOMERS

EMPLOYMENT
GRAPHIC SERVICE   ABOUT US   CONTACT US
OPTIMO
CUSTOMERS

FONT
MAIL   ORDER
OPTIMO™
CLUB   LINKS
WEAR

FLEXO FLEXO FLEXO FLEXO FLEXO FLEXO

OPTIMO

address	www.optimo.ch
concept	Swiss design duo Optimo make perfect use of the online medium. Their dynamic site is an ever evolving forum consisting of a type foundry, an image bank, a sound bank and a collection of links still under construction. As well as looking good, Optimo is an e-commerce site – the designers sell their fonts, clothes and images online. Perhaps best of all, Optimo allows the user to try before they buy using imaginative online showcases. Their experiments with fonts are particularly impressive, as is the accompanying sound.
credits	Design and programming: Gilles Gavillet and David Rust
software	CyberCrazy

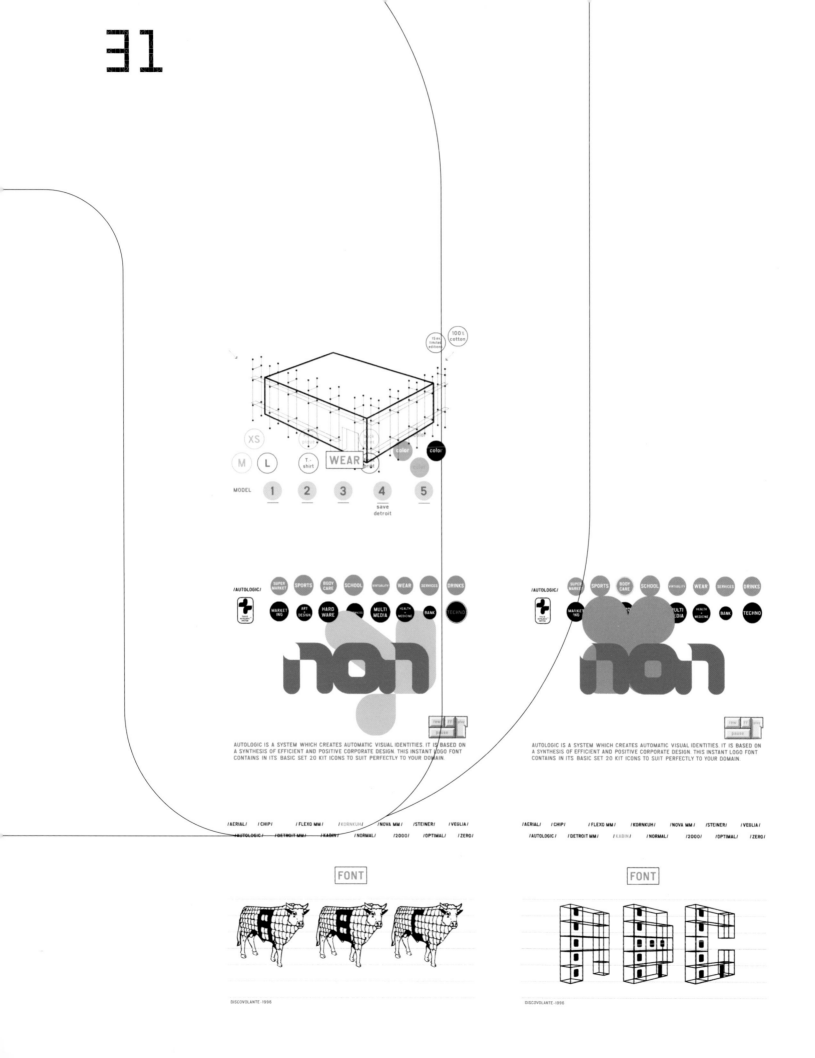

AUTOLOGIC IS A SYSTEM WHICH CREATES AUTOMATIC VISUAL IDENTITIES. IT IS BASED ON A SYNTHESIS OF EFFICIENT AND POSITIVE CORPORATE DESIGN. THIS INSTANT LOGO FONT CONTAINS IN ITS BASIC SET 20 KIT ICONS TO SUIT PERFECTLY TO YOUR DOMAIN.

AUTOLOGIC IS A SYSTEM WHICH CREATES AUTOMATIC VISUAL IDENTITIES. IT IS BASED ON A SYNTHESIS OF EFFICIENT AND POSITIVE CORPORATE DESIGN. THIS INSTANT LOGO FONT CONTAINS IN ITS BASIC SET 20 KIT ICONS TO SUIT PERFECTLY TO YOUR DOMAIN.

/AERIAL/   /CHIP/   /FLEXO MM/   /KORNKUH/   /NOVA MM/   /STEINER/   /VEGLIA/
/AUTOLOGIC/   /DETROIT MM/   /KABIN/   /NORMAL/   /2000/   /OPTIMAL/   /ZERO/

/AERIAL/   /CHIP/   /FLEXO MM/   /KORNKUH/   /NOVA MM/   /STEINER/   /VEGLIA/
/AUTOLOGIC/   /DETROIT MM/   /KABIN/   /NORMAL/   /2000/   /OPTIMAL/   /ZERO/

FONT

FONT

DISCOVOLANTE·1996

DISCOVOLANTE·1996

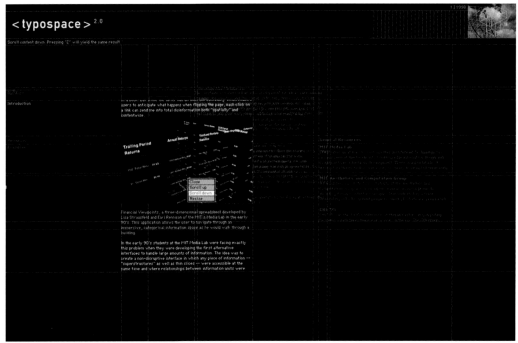

Thomas Noller

↙   www.typospace.de

TYPOSPACE

address	**www.typospace.de**
concept	Unlike real space which is continuous and has no boundaries, web space remains frustratingly fragmented and linear, our experiences online disrupted as we wait for page after page to load. Thomas Noller wants designers to create cyberspace rather than a cybersurface. His site surveys and collects developments and ideas that may be stepping stones to a more dynamic experience, replacing point, click interaction with a more natural type of continuous transition.
credits	Concept, design and programming: Thomas Noller
software	Photoshop, BBEdit

Danny Brown

→   www.amaze.co.uk/noodlebox

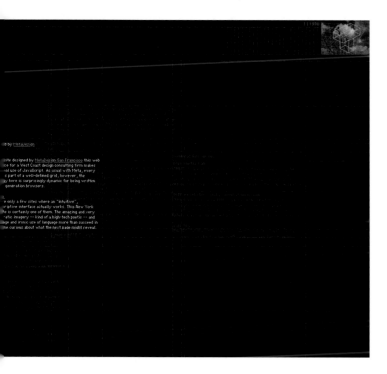

What are your recommended websites?

www.cnet.com
www.fuse98.com
www.audi-tt.com
www.code-design.com
www.suction.com

What single thing would most improve the web from a creative/design point of view?

Alpha channels and transparency.

What is the future of the website in terms of design?

Websites will hopefully move away from imitating print and will define their own rules and possibilities. Too many sites, even the so-called cool ones, still use old print-making aesthetics. This is of course due to the fact that most web designers nowadays have a classic (print-oriented) design education. The next generation will set the standards for this media, not ours.

What will be the next big design trend in websites?

Short-term: everything will be Flash or some other product published by Macromedia. Long-term: HTML-text and simplicity will play a bigger role again. Information is what counts after all.

What are your recommended websites?

www.theremediproject.com
www.colorsmagazine.com
www.io360.com/v2/yo/iogami
www.vapour.org
www.creation.co.uk

What single thing would most improve the web from a creative/design point of view?

Better communication between technical people and creative people. It seems to me in a lot of ways that the problem is everyone blaming the tools at the moment. People are already saying things like 'oh, it doesn't do this or that' about Shockwave for Director 7.0, yet nobody actually used Shockwave 6.0 to anywhere near its full potential. It's not accurate to suggest that the designers are the 'creatives' and the programmers just do what they are told. In a lot of ways, it's reversed: the programmers are the ones who really know what the computer is capable of and ways to optimize visual effects to really kick, whereas the creatives only know how to draw pretty pictures – not exactly useful given bandwidth restrictions. So I really think the thing to improve most is the communication between both sides at the design stage.

ヌードル ボックス

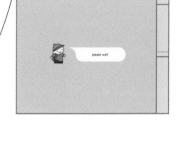

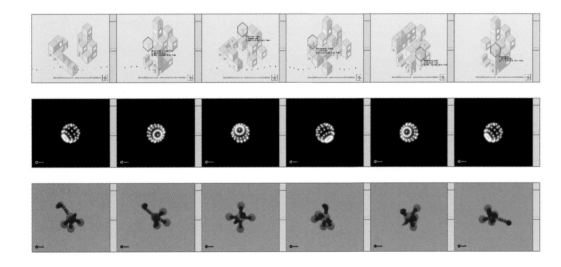

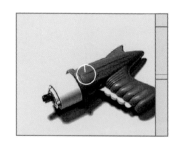

Glowing ball
glowball.dcr
Not visited this time

NOODLEBOX

address   www.amaze.co.uk/noodlebox

concept   Creator Danny Brown calls Noodlebox 'a wake-up call'. Instead of complaining
           about lack of bandwidth and inadequate technologies, Brown says he wanted to
           explore the limits of today's web. The site is a play area which presents a variety
           of fun diversions that have the serious aim of illustrating that, with a little
           thought, the tools currently available to web designers can produce a truly
           immersive environment.

credits   Concept, design and programming: Daniel Brown
           Creative feedback: Roy Stringer and the Amaze team – Tom Hobbs and Lloyd

software   Photoshop, Illustrator, Navigator, BBEdit, Director and 'a few other things'

36

CASA ELECTRONICS

POSTPET
www.sony.com.sg/postpet

PostPet

SMALL ICONIC BITMAP CHARACTERS WILL RULE

LEO MISENHEIMER - 0?

VOLUMEONE
www.volumeone.com

Matt Owens

What are your recommended websites?

What single thing would most improve the web from a creative/design point of view?

What is the future of the website in terms of design?

What will be the next big design trend in websites?

STAMEN
www.stamen.com

Eric Rodenbeck

What are your recommended websites?

What single thing would most improve the web from a creative/design point of view?

What is the future of the website in terms of design?

What will be the next big design trend in websites?

EKIONA
www.ekiona.it

Iigo de Alcala

What are your recommended websites?

What single thing would most improve the web from a creative/design point of view?

What is the future of the website in terms of design?

What will be the next big design trend in websites?

founders'

This is the Remedi Project.

Daniel Jenett

What are your recommended websites?

What single thing would most improve the web from a creative/design point of view?

What is the future of the website in terms of design?

What will be the next big design trend in websites?

REMEDI
www.theremediproject.com

Josh Ulm

What are your recommended websites?

What single thing would most improve the web from a creative/design point of view?

What is the future of the website in terms of design?

What will be the next big design trend in websites?

COMBINE

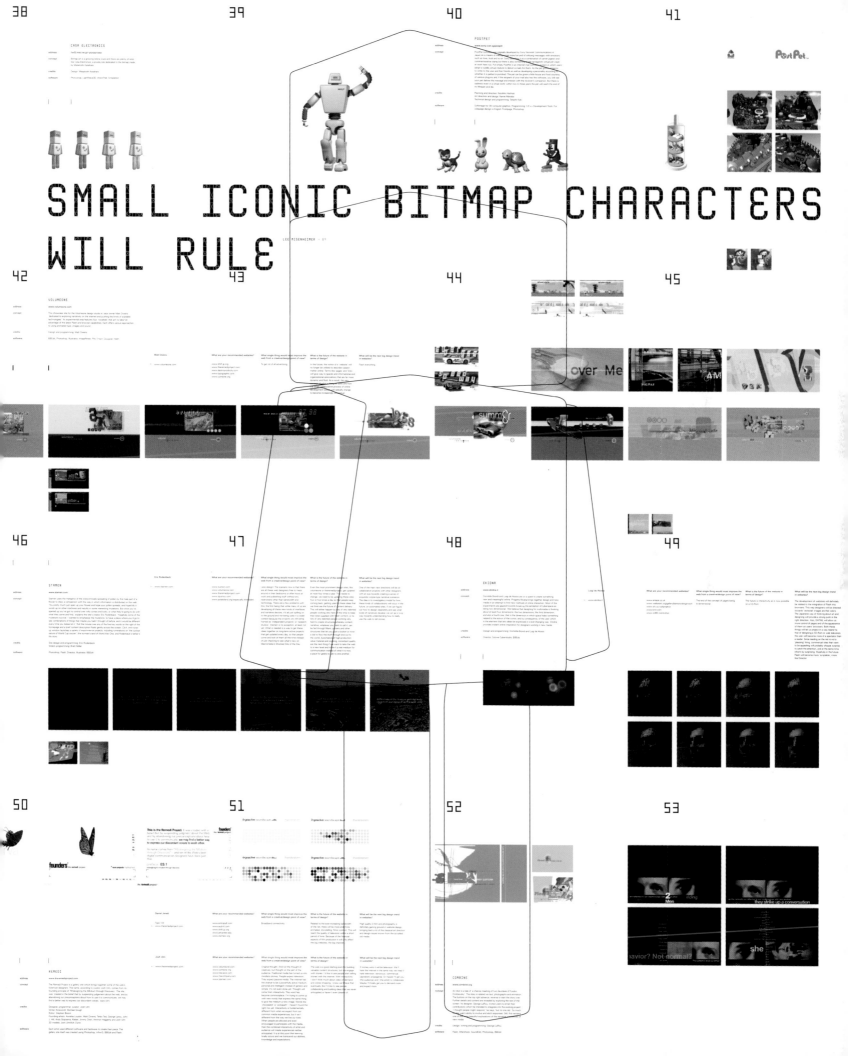

CASA ELECTRONICS

address	//w33.mtci.ne.jp/~piyopy/casa
concept	Bitmap art is a growing online craze and there are plenty of sites like Casa Electronics, a private site dedicated to the bitmap made by Masatoshi Kasahara.
credits	Design: Masatoshi Kasahara
software	Photoshop, LightWave3D, Word Pad, Simpletext

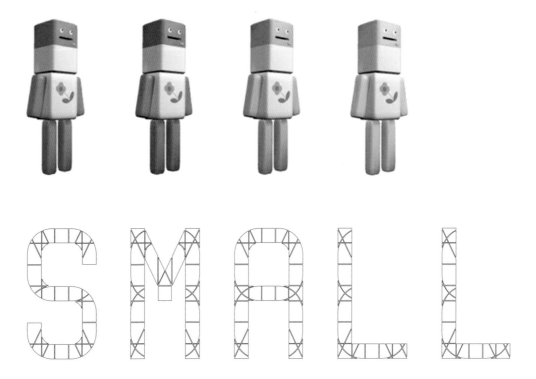

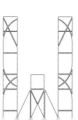 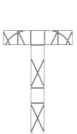   

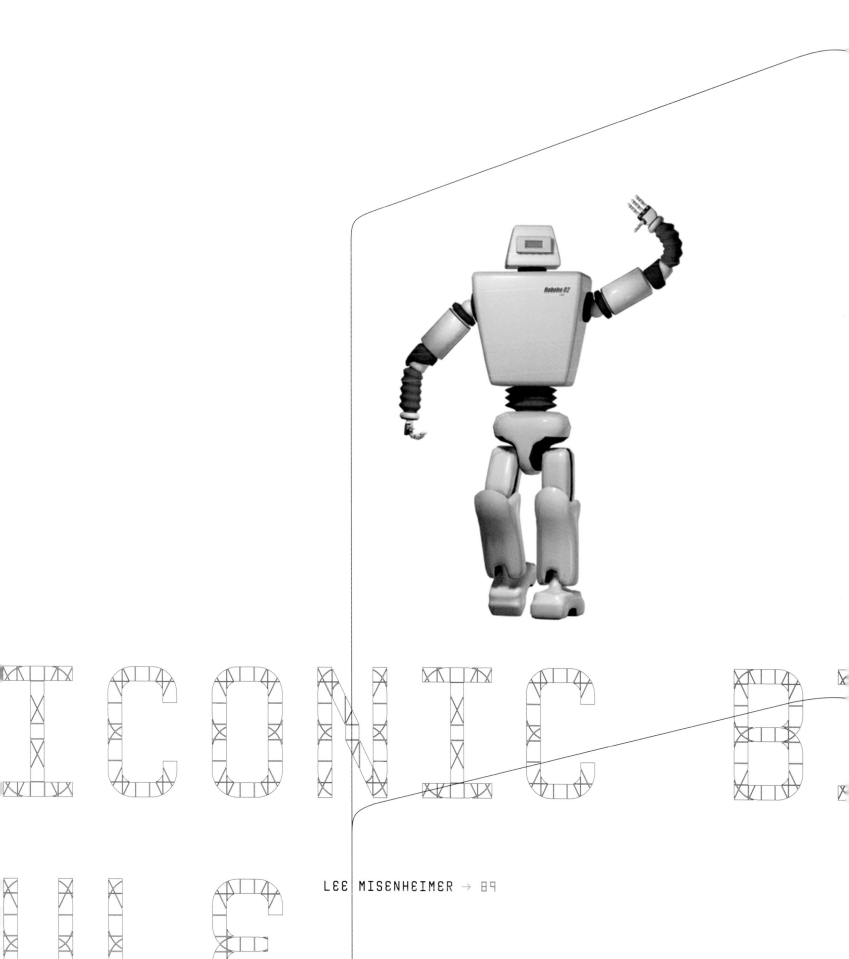

ICONIC B.

LEE MISENHEIMER → 89

IIC.

POSTPET

address

www.sony.com.sg/postpet

concept

PostPet software was originally developed by Sony Network Communications in Japan as a means of making e-mail more fun and of imbuing messages with emotions such as love, trust and so on. Sony describes it as a combination of carrier pigeon and commemorative stamp but there is also something of the tamagotchi virtual pet craze at work here too. Put simply, PostPet is an internet mail software system in which users adopt a cuddly virtual creature to deliver e-mails for them. As the pet grows, it learns to write to the user and their friends as well as developing a personality according to whether it is patted or punished. The pet can be given a little house and food courtesy of various plug-ins and, if the recipient of your mail also has the software, you will see your pet deliver the message and interact with the receiver's companion. But there is sadness even in a virtual world: within two to three years the pet will reach the end of its lifespan and die.

credits

Planning and direction: Kazuhiko Hachiya
Art direction and design: Namie Manabe
Technical design and programming: Takashi Koki

software

Softimage for 3D computer graphics. Programming: C/C++ Development Tools. For webpage design in English: Frontpage, Photoshop

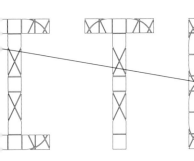
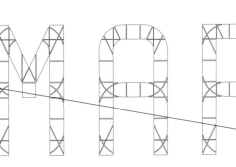
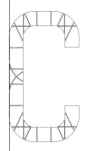
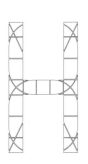

HOME

PostPet™

RACTERS

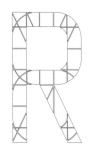
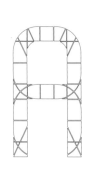
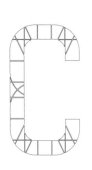
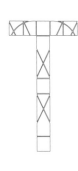
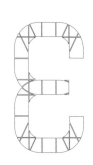
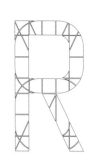
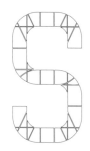

VOLUMEONE

address	www.volumeone.com
concept	This showcase site for the Volumeone design studio is, says owner Matt Owens 'dedicated to exploring narrativity on the internet and pushing the limits of available technologies'. Its experimental area features four 'novelties' that aim to take full advantage of the latest Flash and browser capabilities. Each offers various approaches to using animated type, images and sound.
credits	Design and programming: Matt Owens
software	BBEdit, Photoshop, Illustrator, ImageReady, Ray Dream Designer, Flash

Matt Owens

↖ www.volumeone.com

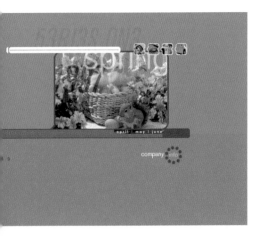

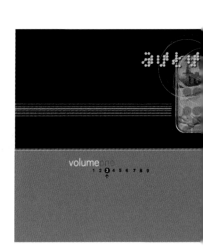

What are your recommended websites?

www.shift.jp.org
www.theremediproject.com
www.destroyrockcity.com
www.typographic.com
www.combine.org

What single thing would most improve the web from a creative/design point of view?

To get rid of all advertising.

What is the future of the website in terms of design?

In the future, the notion of a 'website' will no longer be utilized to describe subject matter online. Terms like 'pages' and 'links' will give way to spaces and informational and organizational associations that are far more dynamic and fluid. As a result, the very concept of what a designer does and how the larger collaborative process of online development occurs will radically change to become increasingly conceptual.

What will be the next big design trend in websites?

Flash everything.

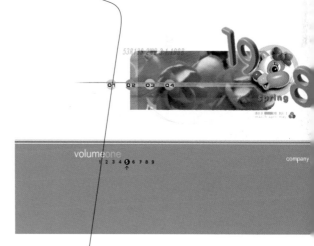

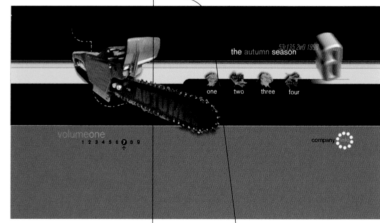

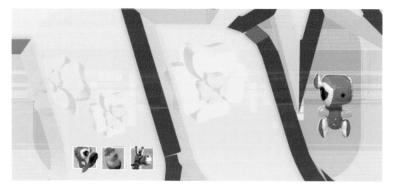

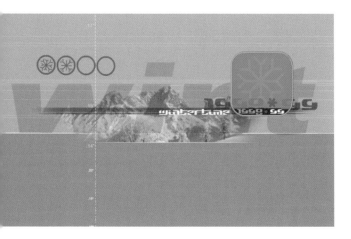

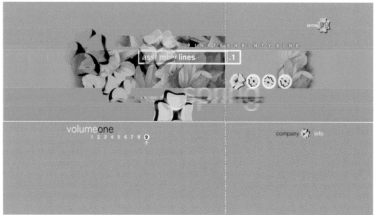

Eric Rodenbeck

STAMEN

← www.stamen.com

address	www.stamen.com
concept	Stamen uses the metaphor of the indiscriminate spreading of pollen by the male part of a flower to draw a comparison with the way in which information is distributed on the web. 'You pretty much just open up your flower and hope your pollen spreads, and hopefully it winds up on other machines and results in some interesting mutations. But once you've opened up you've got no control over who comes and looks, or what they're going to do with what they come and find,' explains the site's creator Eric Rodenbeck. 'Hopefully some of the mutations survive. I wanted to emphasize the mutations, to have a place where you'd go to see combinations of things that maybe you hadn't thought of before, and it would be different every time you looked at it.' Roll the mouse over any of the five key words on the right of the homepage and a brief content description floats gently across the screen. Click, and a pop-up window launches a variety of experimental projects, including ruminations on 'the cyclical nature of World Cup soccer', the no-man's land of World War One, and Rodenbeck's father's life story.
credits	Site design and programming: Eric Rodenbeck Sliders programming: Brett Miller
software	Photoshop, Flash, Director, Illustrator, BBEdit

The term "no-man's land" was invented
to describe the area in between opposing
trenches during the first world war

What are your recommended websites?

www.suction.com
www.volumeone.com
www.theremediproject.com
www.spumco.com
www.potatoland.org [especially /shredder]

What single thing would most improve the web from a creative/design point of view?

Less design! The scenario now is that there are all these web designers free to mess around in their bedrooms or after hours at work and publishing stuff without any restrictions other than bandwidth and technology. There are a few problems with this, the first being that while many of us are developing all these new kinds of interfaces and narrative devices, it's all just spilling on to the ground and not being used in a wider context because the projects are still being framed as 'independent projects' or 'research studios'. Stamen is no exception, at least not yet. What is needed is a way to get these ideas together on long-term active projects that get updated every day, so that people come and look at them all the time instead of just checking to see what's new on Macromedia's Shocked Site of the Day.

What is the future of the website in terms of design?

Even the most prominent design sites, like volumeone or theremediproject, get updated at most four times a year. This needs to change; we need to be updating these sites four or five times a day so that people keep coming back, getting used to these ideas that we think are the future of content delivery. This will either happen by lots of very talented people working very hard all the time to keep their sites supplied with fresh content, or by lots of very talented people working very hard to create structures whereby content, narrative, whatever you want to call it, can be fed through filters, parsers and other structures that let you push a button or twist a dial to flow the stuff through and out to the world. Automation of high-production-value material and ongoing, consistent quality are the next thing if we want to take the web to a new level and make it a real medium for communication instead of what it is now, a place for geeks to talk to one another.

What will be the next big design trend in websites?

One of the main new directions will be on collaborative projects with other designers, with an eye towards creating a series of exquisite corpse-type narrative scenarios. The idea is to investigate a model for how these kinds of collaborations will occur in the future, on automated sites; if we can figure out how to design separately and see what kinds of narratives develop we can go a long way towards understanding how to really use the web to tell stories.

these landscapes illustrate the new nature of industrial warfare at the beginning of the twentieth century

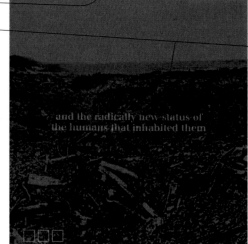

and the radically new status of the humans that inhabited them

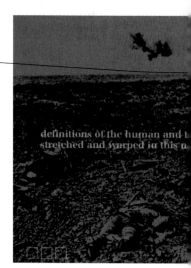

definitions of the human and t
stretched and warped in this n

EKIDNA

address	www.ekidna.it
concept	Domitilla Biondi and Luigi de Aloisio are on a quest to create something new and meaningful online. Progetto Ekidna brings together design and new media in an attempt to find new methods of online interaction. Most of the experiments are geared towards breaking the perception of cyberspace as being two dimensional. 'We believe that designing for multimedia is thinking about at least four dimensions: the two dimensions, the third dimension, and also a fourth one, that is the dimension in which space hides something related to the action of the cursor, and by consequence, of the user which is the element that lets ideas be expressed in a ever-changing way.' Ekidna provides instant online inspiration for designers working in new media.
credits	Design and programming: Domitilla Biondi and Luigi de Aloisio
software	Director, GoLive Cyberstudio, BBEdit

Luigi de Aloisio

← www.ekidna.it

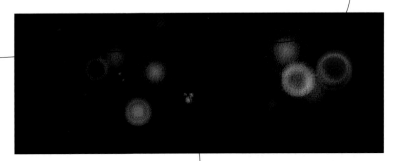

body zone

What are your recommended websites?

www.amaze.co.uk
www.walkerart.org/gallery9/artists/dingansich
www.sfx.co.nz/tamahori
www.brnr.com
www.io360.com/v2/yo

What single thing would most improve the web from a creative/design point of view?

The end of the concept of pages being bi-dimensional.

What is the future of the website in terms of design?

The future is interactivity as is now possible on a CD-Rom.

What will be the next big design trend in websites?

The development of websites will definitely be related to the integration of Flash into browsers. This way designers will be directed towards 'vectorial' images and flat colors. The Japanese way of thinking about art and designing will provide a strong push in the right direction. Also, DHTML will allow us more control of pages and of the appearance of them on users' browsers. Both these things will let us project in a way nearer to that of designing a CD-Rom or web television: the user will become more of a spectator than a reader. Since reading on the net is not a 'pleasing' thing, commercial sites that want to be appealing will probably choose surprise to catch the attention, and at the same time inform by surprising. Hopefully in the future Flash will become more 'scriptable', more like Director.

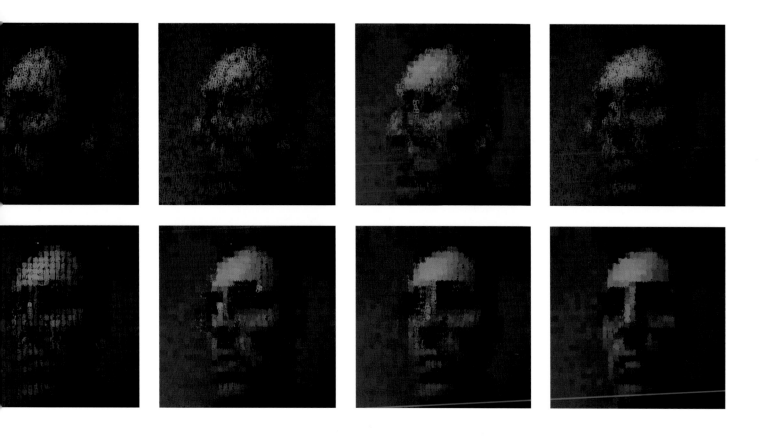

larva

01.
02.
03.
14.

15.
00.

0.

founders' the remedi project   * **new projects** highlighted

04. 05. 06. 07. 08. 09. 10. 11. 12. 13.

the remedi project

This is the Remedi Project. It was
belief that by suspending judgment
and by abandoning our preconceptio
to use it to communicate, **we may fin**
to express our discordant voices to

Its name comes from "REdesigning
through DIscovery" -- and ten of the
digital communication designers hav
that.

preface **03.1**
redesigning the medium through discovery

the **remedi** project
programme   founders   fm15   information   merchandise

Daniel Jenett

Typo 123
← www.theremediproject.com

Josh Ulm

← www.theremediproject.com

REMEDI

address	www.theremediproject.com
concept	The Remedi Project is a gallery site which brings together some of the web's foremost designers. The name, according to curator Josh Ulm, comes from its founding principle of 'REdesigning the MEdium through DIscovery'. The site was 'created in the belief that by suspending judgement about the web, and by abandoning our preconceptions about how to use it to communicate, we may find a better way to express our discordant voices,' says Ulm.
credits	Designer, programmer, curator: Josh Ulm Writer (foreword): Michael Gough Editor: Stephen Bloom Founding artists: Annette Loudon, Matt Owens, Terbo Ted, George Larou, John J. Hill, Andy Slopsema, Kleber, Jimmy Chen, Ammon Haggerty and Josh Ulm 3D models: Josh Ulm/Kirk Clyne
software	Each artist used different software and hardware to create their piece. The gallery site itself was created using Photoshop, Infini-D, BBEdit and Flash.

ěrgoactive soundscape ▪▫▫▫▫▫ thunderstorm   ěrgoactive soundscape ▪▫▪▫▫ thunderstorm

founders'
the **remedi** project

h a
Web,
how
way

m
st
t

01.
02.
03.
14.

15.
00.

0.

.1 .2 .3 .4

06. 07. 08. 09. 10. 11. 12. 13.

ěrgoactive soundscape ▪▫▪▫▫ thunderstorm   ěrgoactive soundscape ▪▫▫▫▫ thunderstorm

What are your recommended websites?

www.entropy8.com
www.audi-tt.com
www.shift.jp.org
www.artcenter.edu
www.olympic.org

What single thing would most improve the web from a creative/design point of view?

Broadband connectivity.

What is the future of the website in terms of design?

Related to the ever-increasing bandwidth of the net, there will be more and more animated, storytelling, filmic content. This will reach the quality of television within a short period of time. Because of the financial aspects of film production it will only affect the big websites, the big channels.

What will be the next big design trend in websites?

High quality in film and photography is definitely gaining ground in website design, bringing back a lot of the classical art direction and design issues known from the so-called old media.

What are your recommended websites?

www.volumeone.com
www.combine.org
www.tree-axis.com
www.mecompany.com
www.stamen.com

What single thing would most improve the web from a creative/design point of view?

Original thought. And not the thought of creatives, but thought on the part of the audience. Traditional media has turned us into mindless drones. People expect television. They expect passive media. The internet has the chance to be a powerfully active medium, personal and intelligent instead of generic and simple. It's not even close yet. Thought will come from interactivity. This word has become commonplace. I'm trying to come up with new words that express the same thing to give the medium a new image. Words like 'choosealot' or 'pickapath': I haven't found the right mix yet. Interactivity is fundamentally different from what we expect from our common media experiences, but it isn't different from the way we live our lives. When people are allowed and even encouraged to participate with the media, then the combined interactivity of artist and audience will create experiences neither anticipated. It is at this point that learning finally occurs and we transcend our abilities, knowledge and expectations.

What is the future of the website in terms of design?

The web is a good starting point for building valuable content structures, but we engage with stories. I'd like to see people start telling stories with the internet. With interactivity. I don't think much about video on demand and online shopping. I know we'll have that eventually. But I'd like to see people collaborating and building ideas that we never anticipated or haven't even dreamt of.

What will be the next big design trend in websites?

If money wins it will be television. We'll hate the internet in the same way we (read I) hate television: obnoxious, commercial, capitalistic propaganda. Or maybe I'll get you (the audience) and I (the artist) to collaborate. Maybe I'll finally get you to demand more and expect more.

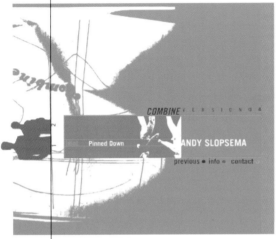

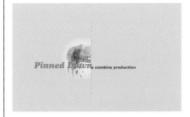

COMBINE

address   www.combine.org

concept   'Welcome to our latest excursion into the realm of visual experimentation', is the message greeting all visitors to combine.org. Simple exploration is the name of the game: as it says on the site, it is 'yours to explore or ignore'. All manner of weird and wonderful things exist on the site and both of combine's creators make regular updates. As it stands, combine.org pushes the boundaries of online design while retaining an all-important sense of humour.

credits   Design, writing and programming: George LaRou, Andy Slopsema

software Flash, Aftershock, SoundEdit, Photoshop, BBEdit

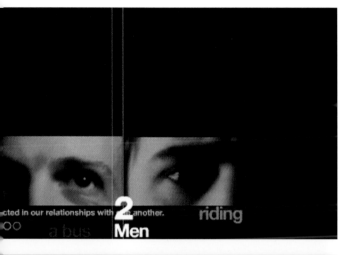

...cted in our relationships with 2 another. riding

a bus **Men**

· up the network are reflected in our relationships with one another.

they strike up a conversation

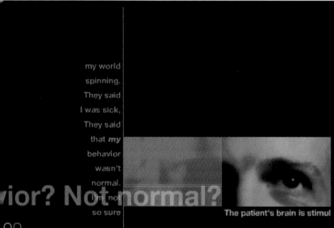

my world
spinning.
They said
I was sick,
They said
that *my*
behavior
wasn't
normal.
so sure

vior? Not normal?

The patient's brain is stimul

story And she
of an knew
unattainable that
gal. none of
She them
knew interested
that all her in t
those he least.
around But
her most
wanted her. importantly
she knew
she
enjoyed
the
power
that
she
had
over
all of

she

54

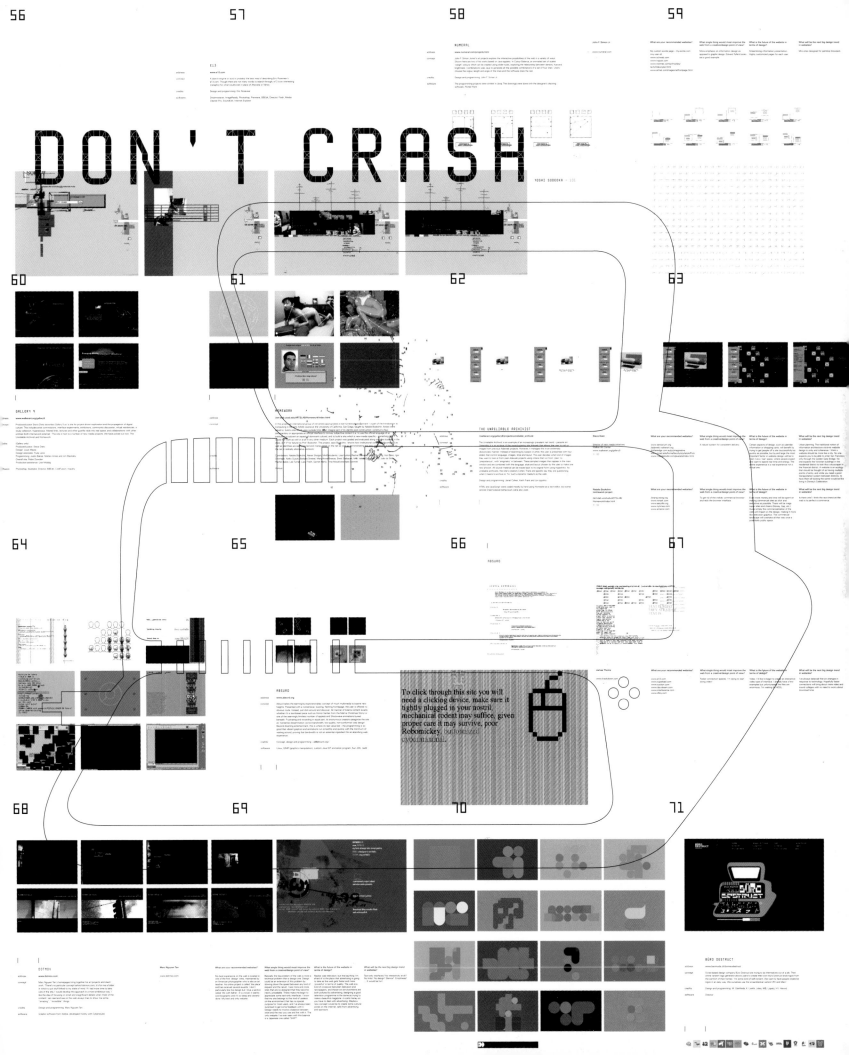

DON'T CRASH

YOSHI SODEOKA – 101

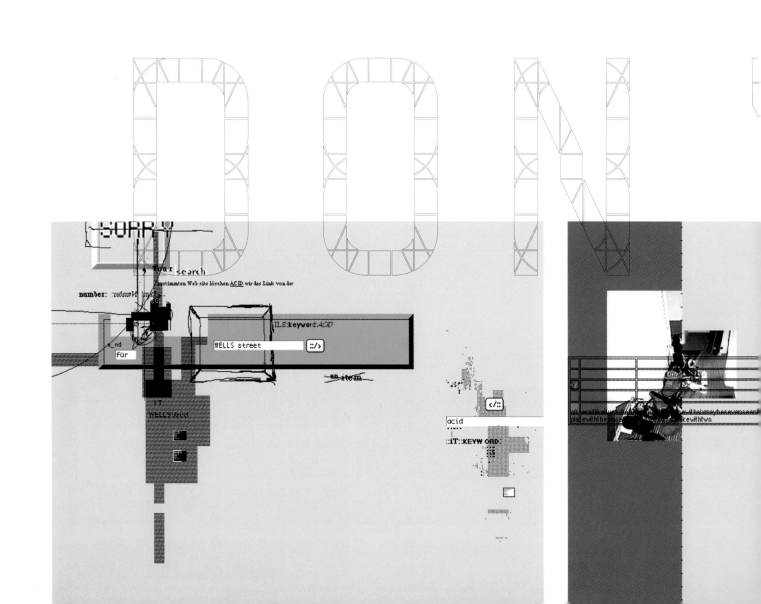

ε13

www.e13.com

A search engine on acid is probably the best way of describing Eric Rosevear's e13.com. Though there are not many words to search through, e13 is an interesting metaphor for what could exist in place of Altavista or Yahoo.

Design and programming: Eric Rosevear

Dreamweaver, ImageReady, Photoshop, Premiere, BBEdit, Director, Flash, Media Cleaner Pro, SoundEdit, Internet Explorer

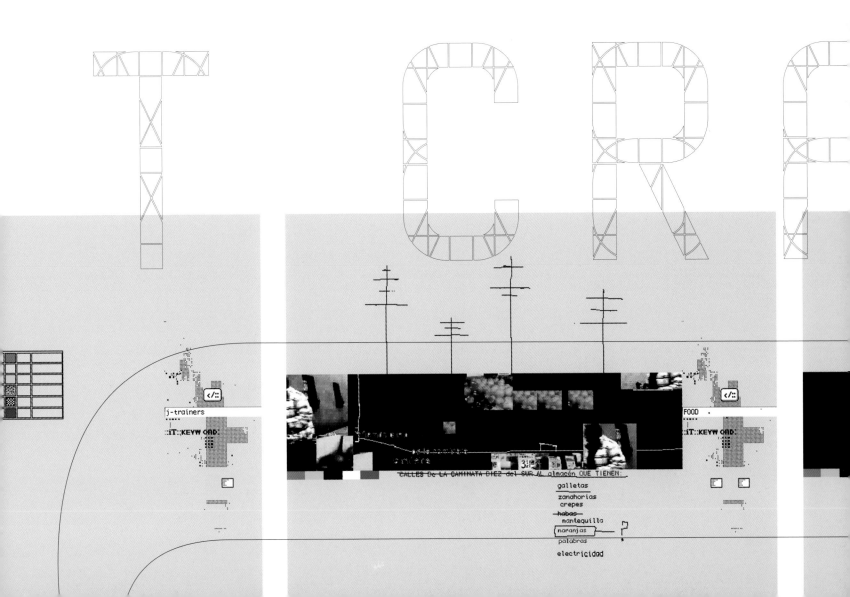

NUMERAL

John F. Simon Jr

address	www.numeral.com/projects.html
concept	John F. Simon Junior's art projects explore the interactive possibilities of the web in a variety of ways. Shown here are two of his works based on Java applets. In Colour Balance, an animated set of scales 'weigh' colours which can be created using slider tools, exploring the relationship between density, hue and brightness. Combinations uses Java to generate all the possible combinations of a set of four lines. Users choose the colour, length and angle of the lines and the software does the rest.
credits	Design and programming: John F. Simon Jr
software	The programming projects were written in Java. The drawings were done with the designer's drawing software, Plotter Paint.

← www.numeral.com

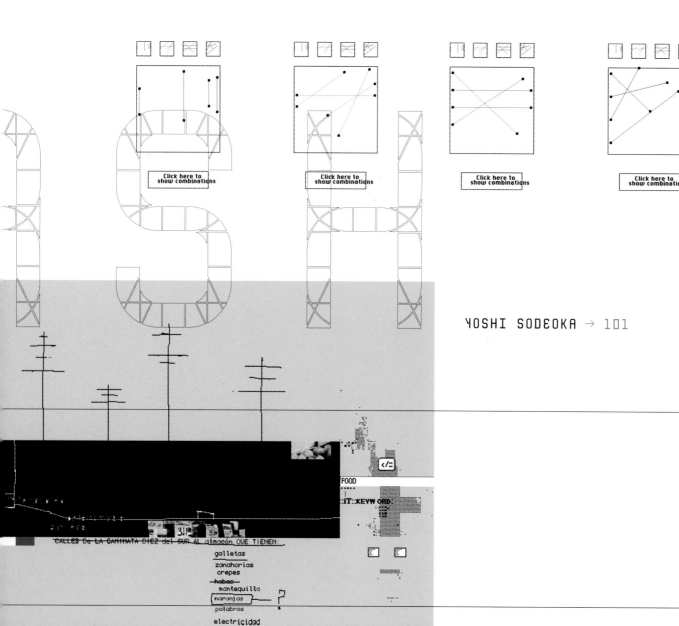

Click here to
show combinations

Click here to
show combinations

Click here to
show combinations

Click here to
show combinations

YOSHI SODEOKA → 101

FOOD

:T::KEYWORD:

CALLES DE LA CAMINATA DIEZ del SUR AL almacén QUE TIENEN:

galletas
zanahorias
crepes
habas
mantequilla
naranjas ?
palabras
electricidad

What are your recommended websites?

My custom excite page – my.excite.com
(my user id)
www.schwab.com
www.nypost.com
www.nytimes.com/yr/mo/day/
tech/indexcyber.html
www.artnet.com/magazine/frontpage.html

What single thing would most improve the web from a creative/design point of view?

More emphasis on information design as opposed to graphic design. Edward Tufte's books set a good example.

What is the future of the website in terms of design?

Streamlining information presentation. Highly customized pages for each user.

What will be the next big design trend in websites?

Mini-sites designed for palmtop browsers.

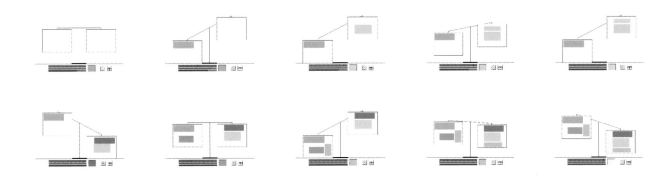

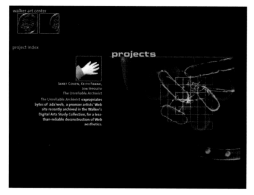

GALLERY 9

address   www.walkerart.org/gallery9

concept   Producer/curator Steve Dietz describes Gallery 9 as 'a site for project-driven exploration and the propagation of digital culture. This includes artist commissions, interface experiments, exhibitions, community discussion, virtual residencies, a study collection, hyperessays, filtered links, lectures and other guerilla raids into real space, and collaborations with other entities (both internal and external).' The site is host to a number of new media projects. We have picked out two: The Unreliable Archivist and Homework.

credits   (Gallery only)
Producer/curator: Steve Dietz
Design: Louis Mazza
Design associate: Trudy Lane
Programming: Justin Bakse, Matteo Ames and Jim Blackaby
Overall site: Robin Dowden
Production assistance: Lisa Middag

software   Photoshop, Illustrator, Director, BBEdit, ColdFusion, Inquery

Fools are my
theme, let satire
be my song.

—Lord Byron

Brasilian artist and poet João da Silva travels in Europe

Great Britain

- Would you like to sleep with me?

HOMEWORK

address

//art-slab.ucsd.edu/ARTSLAB/Homework/index.html

concept

In this project an international group of net artists appropriated a real homework assignment – a part of the Introduction to Computing in the Arts (VA40) course at the University of California, San Diego, taught by Natalie Bookchin. Artists were asked to: build a site which uses outside links as an integral part of its identity and construction; construct a faux documentary or appropriate an official interface to convey subjective content (i.e. to use the official language of an institution to subvert an aspect of dominant culture); and to build a site which is new-media specific – something that would not work as well or at all in any other medium. Each project was graded and evaluated along with the students in the class, A–F (F for failure) by Prof. Bookchin. The project, says Bookchin, 'shows how institutional constraints/ boundaries as well as identities are easily blurred and manipulated on the net as well as demonstrating the easy movement of artists on the net in radically alternative contexts'.

Contributors: Natalie Bookchin, Alexei Shulgin, VA40 students, Lisa Hutton, Rachel Stevens, Heath Bunting, Vuk Cosic, Igor Stromajer, Keiko Suzuki, Barbara Strebel, Mary-Anne Breeze, Brett Stalbaum, M@, Valery Grancher, jodi, João da Silva, Rachel Baker, Lee Turner, Luka Frelih, Garnet Hertz, Trina Mould and Kass Schmitt

credits

software

Various

6

5

4

home

3

2 1 2 2 3 4 5 6
7 8
9
10

5 6 11
4 7
12

3 13
8
4
5 2

THE UNRELIABLE ARCHIVIST

1 9 14
address
15
concept 10
8 16
31 17
7 30 18
29 19
28 20
6 21
5 27 22
26 24
25 23

credits

software

6

//walkerart.org/gallery9/projects/unreliable_archivist

The Unreliable Archivist is an example of an increasingly prevalent net trend – parasite art. Ostensibly it is an archive of the award-winning site Adaweb that allows the user to call up images from previous Adaweb projects. However, it manages this in an extremely idiosyncratic manner. Instead of searching by subject or artist, the user is presented with four sliders that control language, images, style and layout. The user decides what kind of images they want to look at from past Adaweb projects using criteria that run from 'plain' to 'preposterous', with 'enigmatic' in between. These sampled images then appear in the main window and are combined with the language, style and layout chosen by the user to make one new artwork. All source material can be traced back to its original form using hyperlinks. As unreliable archivists, the site's creators Cohen, Frank and Ippolito say they are questioning what it means to archive or 'fix' such a dynamic medium as the web.

Design and programming: Janet Cohen, Keith Frank and Jon Ippolito

HTML and JavaScript were coded mostly by hand using Homesite as a text editor, but some canned Dreamweaver behaviours were also used.

Steve Dietz

director of new media initiatives, Walker Art Center
www.walkerart.org/gallery9
← 60

Natalie Bookchin
Homework project

//art-slab.ucsd.edu/ARTSLAB/
Homework/index.html
← 61

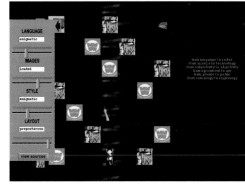

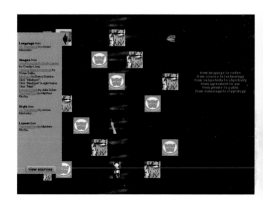

What are your recommended websites?

www.sensorium.org
//adaweb.walkerart.org
//otheredge.com.au/prj/imaginative
www.mcad.edu/home/faculty/szyhalski/Piotr
www.maedastudio.com/javacals/index.html

What single thing would most improve the web from a creative/design point of view?

A robust system for consistent delivery.

What is the future of the website in terms of design?

Certain aspects of design, such as calendar information or shopping carts, will benefit by trying to get people off a site (successfully) as quickly as possible, but by and large the most important factor in website design will be to treat it as a 'real' space, where people expect and want to spend real time and energy. The online experience is a real experience not a virtual one.

What will be the next big design trend in websites?

Urban planning. The traditional notion of information architecture vis-à-vis website design is unity and coherence. I think a website should be more like a city. No one expects you to be able to enter San Francisco only through the Golden Gate Bridge. No one expects the Victorian buildings in the residential district to look like a skyscraper in the financial district. A website is an ecology that should be thought of as having multiple points of entry, and while you need a good transportation system between districts, to have them all looking the same would be like living in Disney's Celebration.

What are your recommended websites?

//orang.orang.org
www.rtmark.com
www.easylife.org
www.nytimes.com
www.amazon.com

What single thing would most improve the web from a creative/design point of view?

To get rid of the visible, commercial browser and redo the browser interface.

What is the future of the website in terms of design?

Even more money and time will be spent on making commercial sites as slick and seductive as possible. There will be mega super sites and chains (Disney, Gap, etc.). Quite simply the commercialization of the web will impact on the design, making it more like television graphics. The commercial landscape will overtake all that was once a potentially public space.

What will be the next big design trend in websites?

Is there one? I think the next trend on the web is to perfect e.commerce.

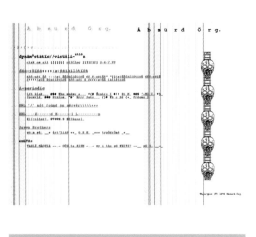

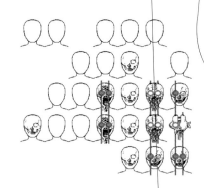

⁰dÊÊ >>> generÄtion zeite   IS

¹grÄBBing them by   their eyeballs

²pound down on   your BRAIN

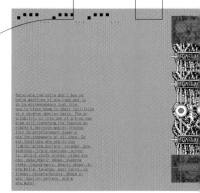

Would you be Intere
>:26_% 8 <0&# in
increasing your Online
WebsiCLXCKte aa;kdj;;;;
Business 3242 993 Sales
by up to 4000.0000% through
:&_forFREE?<}]
70 &9-?]: sales ON <>
onlignlinenenonline
7:9.~~:**?386 _+!!%!~
`5>]sa$`les
1#{08}&THEM =88}_]1%~)<0&#;$!2
(-)>:26_% 8!`3^92 3 send it alo
ng !!%!< post
marked by7>7 &=}<>?
6}·0%ALL{#+
02$@@-> 1#%0!8 with payment>1*$)73:}{ 234230 99 form of
Online (&%&!!%!<)tising
for FREE?

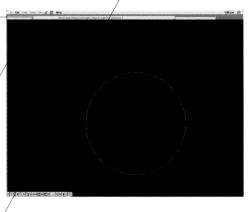

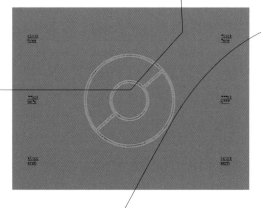

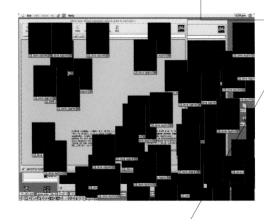

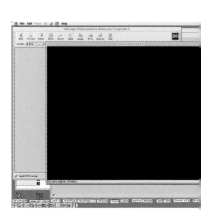

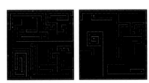

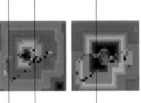

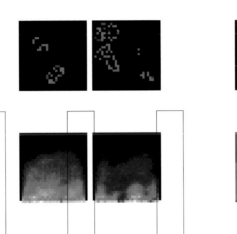

ABSURD

address   www.absurd.org

concept   Absurd takes the learning-by-exploration/play concept of much multimedia to bizarre new heights. Presented with a nonsensical, buzzing, flashing homepage, the user is offered no obvious route. Instead, just click around and discover. All manner of bizarre content awaits, whether it's a text-based piece such as Horror Santas from the Mall (a Christmas Story) or one of the seemingly limitless number of applets and Shockwave animations buried beneath. Frustrating and rewarding in equal part, its anonymous creators categorize the site as 'nonsense dissemination via low-bandwidth, low-quality, non-conformist web design'. Beyond diverting entertainment, this is where its real value lies – the programming is so good that vibrant graphics and animations run smoothly and quickly with the minimum of waiting around, proving that bandwidth is not an essential ingredient for an absorbing web experience.

credits   Concept, design and programming: <a@absurd.org>

software   Linux, GIMP (graphics manipulation), custom Java GIF animation program, Sun JDK, nedit

ABSURD

[J a v v a   B r ö t h e r s]

. . . .

Javva Brothers is an elite group of industry-leading experts specializing in programming on
named-after-coffee-brand™ and **named-after-island**™ languages. **Javva Brothers** have 1000+ man-years of
experience in creating the finest state-of-the-art scaleable-portable object-oriented mission-critical
user-friendly standards-compliant ISO9000-certified award-winning applications available in plug-and-play or
built-in form. Specialists prefer Javva Brothers applications 4 to 1.

. . . [A.P.P.L.I.C.A.T.I.O.N.S] . . . . . .

[X M L]

Acronymical Änti-browsing for Änti-masses

[02-Jun-1998 cre | 1m 16-Jun-1998]

[wörm wår]

Advanced worm navigation in a strangling world of worm warfare.

[07-December-1997 | created]

[art"life]

a finite number of artificial lifeform simulations
activated by applying explicit mouse dragging action (*)

[20-October-1997 | created]

[G. B. M.]

G.B.M. is a Grid Bag Manipulator (of visual type) with built-in code generating engine. It allows to add/delete various controls, modify their
GridBagConstraints on the fly, inspect changes as they made, and instantly generate 100% functional code which can be immediately
copy/pasted into the application.

[06-February-1997 | created]

[t Y p 0 d r ö m e]

Typodrome is an applet which can be used to practice typing skills, or create ones if there aren't any --
with graphs for visualization and self-appreciation.

[10-January-1997 | created]

. . .

[* in association with @bsurd Örg]

WHILE <blink> probably is the most hatred tag
deé-zeigñ would probably look like this

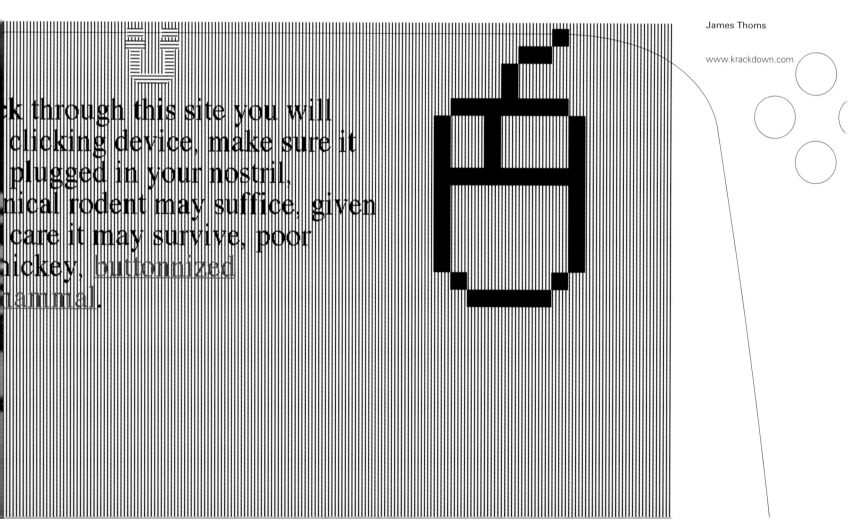

and not-alike, the most fearful piece of HTML

BEWARE OF ...   attention BEWARE

BEWARE OF ...   attention BEWARE
BEWARE OF ...   attention BEWARE !!
BEWARE OF ...   attention BEWARE
BEWARE OF ...   attention BEWARE
BEWARE OF ^^^   attention BEWARE !
BEWARE OF ^^^   attention BEWARE
BEWARE OF ^^^   attention BEWARE
BEWARE OF ...   attention BEWARE

TEXT IS WHAT
THEY AFRAID OF
TEXT IS

diarrhea of diaries:::(@)ântidefithilôtiôñ

sensitive fluffy diaries:::(@)ântidefithilôtiôñ

beautifully written diaries:::(@)ântidefithilôtiôñ

What are your recommended websites?

www.e13.com
www.superbad.com
www.suction.com
www.day-dream.com
www.interference.com
www.dhky.com

What single thing would most improve the web from a creative/design point of view?

Faster connection speeds. I'm dying to start doing video!

What is the future of the website in terms of design?

Video. I'd like to begin to create an interactive video type of interface. I already have a few examples but unfortunately the files are enormous. I'm waiting for ADSL.

What will be the next big design trend in websites?

I've always believed that art changes in response to technology. Hopefully faster connections will bring about more video and sound collages with no need to worry about download time.

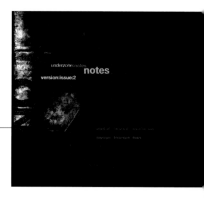

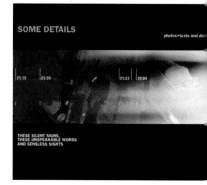

DOTMOV

Marc Nguyen Tan

address www.dotmov.com

← www.dotmov.com

concept Marc Nguyen Tan's homepages bring together his art projects and client work. 'There's no particular concept behind dotmov.com; it's for me a folder in which to put stuff linked to my state of mind. If I had more time to take care of the site, I would develop this approach in a more ambitious way. I like the idea of focusing on small and insignificant details when most of the content I can read and see on the web always tries to show me some "amazing", "incredible" things.'

credits Design and programming: Marc Nguyen Tan

software Graphic software from Adobe, developed mostly with Cyberstudio

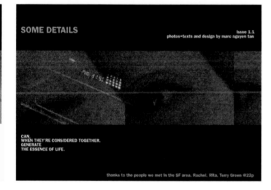

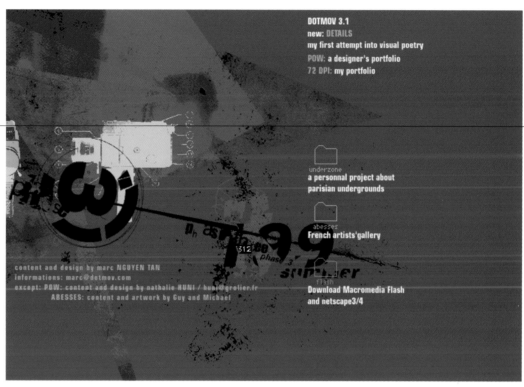

What are your recommended websites?

My best experience on the web is located in one of the first 'design' sites, maintained by an American photographer who is also an art teacher; his online project is called 'the place' and has received several awards; I don't particularly like the design but I love a section called 'life with father'; it's a novel, it seems auto-biographic and it's so deep and cleverly done. My best and only website.

What single thing would most improve the web from a creative/design point of view?

Basically the big problem of the web is more a technical problem than a design one. Design could be an extension of this problem by slowing down the speed between any kind of request and the result; I see more and more sites that are so designed that they become nearly unloadable. These make me begin to appreciate some text-only interfaces. I know that my site belongs to this kind of useless on-line environment that has no special purpose for most users, and I've always been surprised to get some feedback with it. Design needs to involve a balance between style and the way you use and live with it. The only website I've ever seen with this balance is a Japanese one called 'SHIFT'.

What is the future of the website in terms of design?

Maybe web television; but the big thing I'm afraid of is the place that advertising is going to take as the web gets faster and more 'powerful' in terms of quality. The web is a kind of crossover between television and newspapers, and these two environments are both polluted by advertising; designing a good television programme is the same as trying to make a beautiful magazine: it costs money so you have to deal with advertising. Maybe a new concept would be to create some cultural zones on the internet, safe from advertising and sponsors.

What will be the next big design trend in websites?

Text-only interfaces? No interactivity at all? No links? No design? Silence? Emptiness? ... It would be fun!

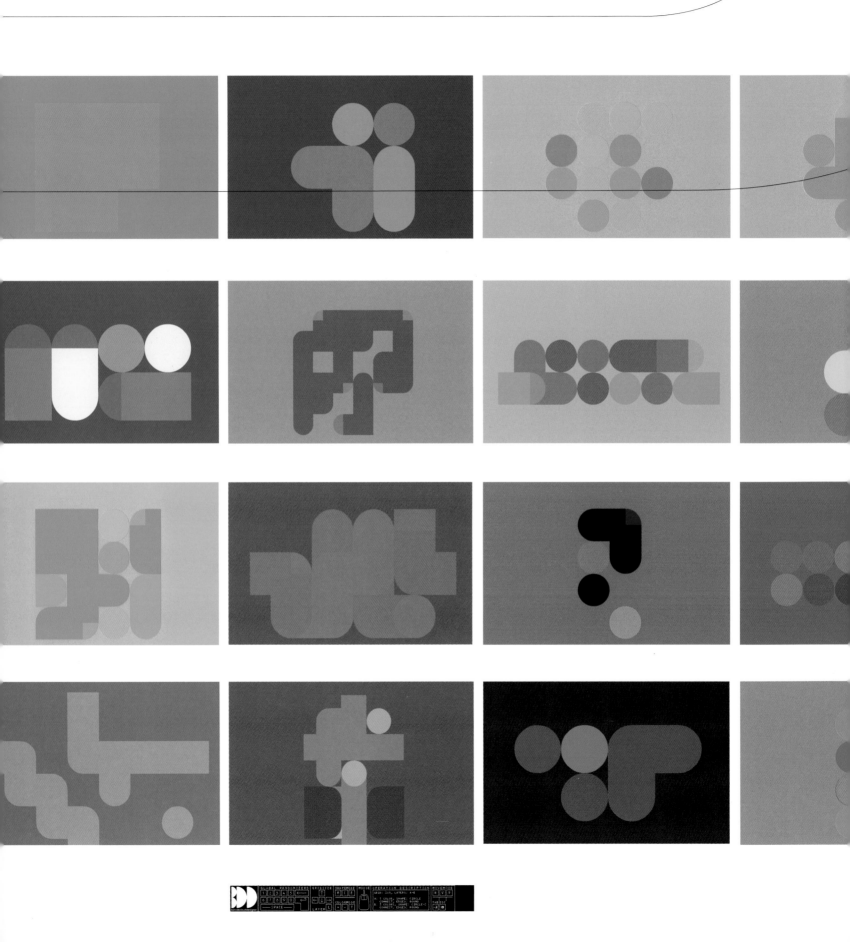

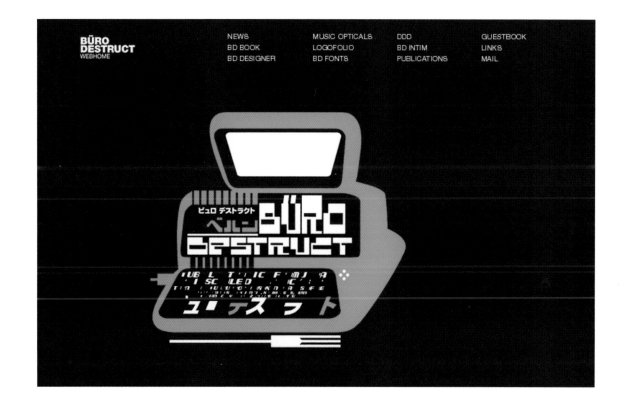

BÜRO DESTRUCT

address	www.bermuda.ch/bureaudestruct
concept	Swiss-based design company Büro Destruct are trying to do themselves out of a job. Their online random logo generator allows users to create their own Büro Destruct-style logos from the comfort of their homes. 'It's some kind of self-ironism. We want to have people create bd logos in an easy way. We ourselves use the screenblanker version (PC and Mac).'
credits	Design and programming: M. Gianfreda, K. Luethi, Jules, MB, Lopetz, H1, Heiwid
software	Director

72

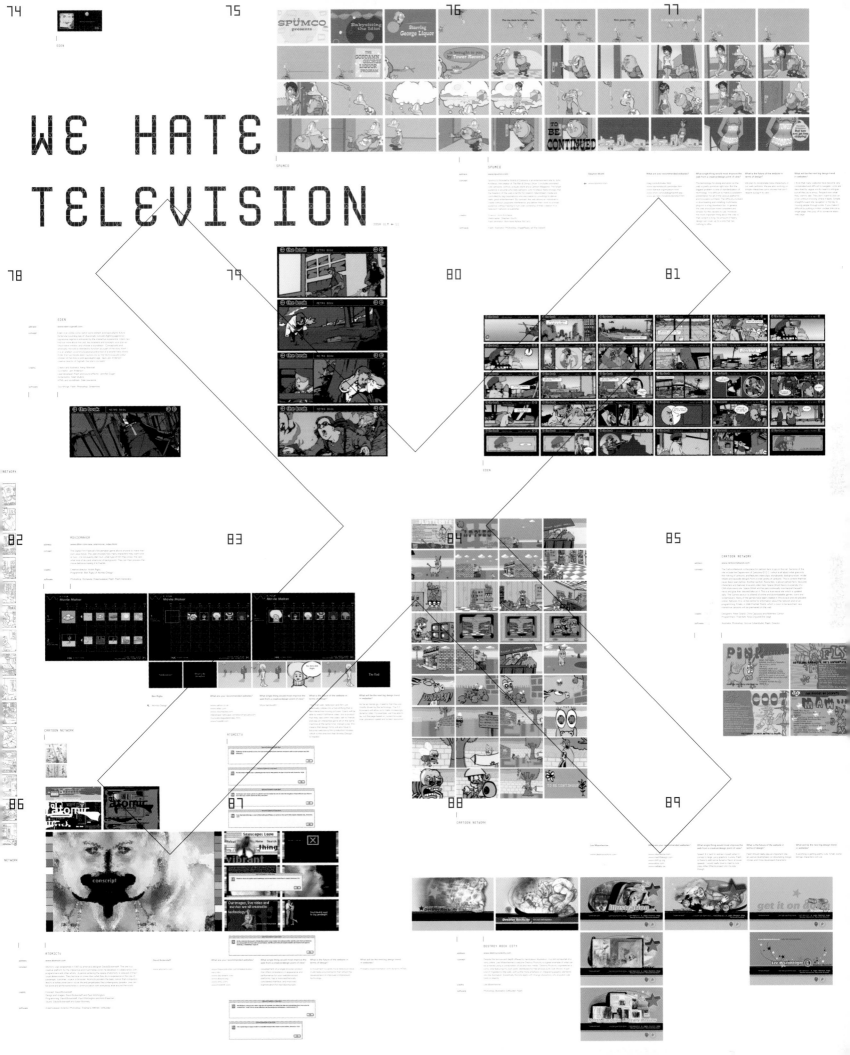

WE HATE
TELEVISION

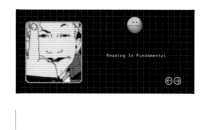

EDEN

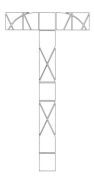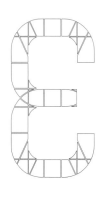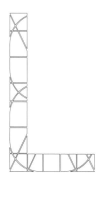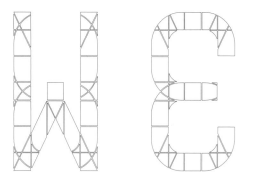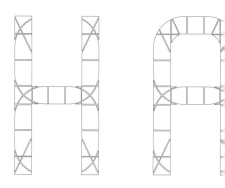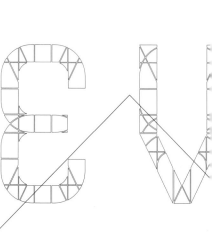

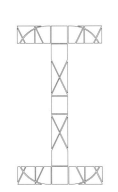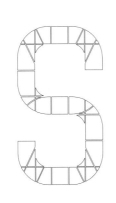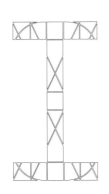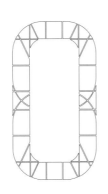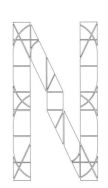

SPUMCO

JOSH ULM ← 51

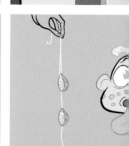

SPUMCO

address	www.spumco.com
concept	Spumco's Wonderful World of Cartoons is an entertainment site by John Kricfalusi, the creator of *The Ren & Stimpy Show*. It includes animated web cartoons, comics, a studio store and a Cartoon Magazine. The target audience is anyone who likes cartoons. John Kricfalusi feels strongly that the freedom of the web is terrific for creators. Mainstream media are controlled by big corporations who are unable (or unwilling) to deliver really good entertainment. By contrast, the web allows an individual to create without corporate interference, and deliver their work to a broad audience without having to turn over ownership of their creation to a television network or publisher.
credits	Director: John Kricfalusi Webmaster: Stephen Worth Flash animator: Annmarie Ashkar McCarty
software	Flash, Illustrator, Photoshop, ImageReady (all Mac-based)

Stephen Worth

← www.spumco.com

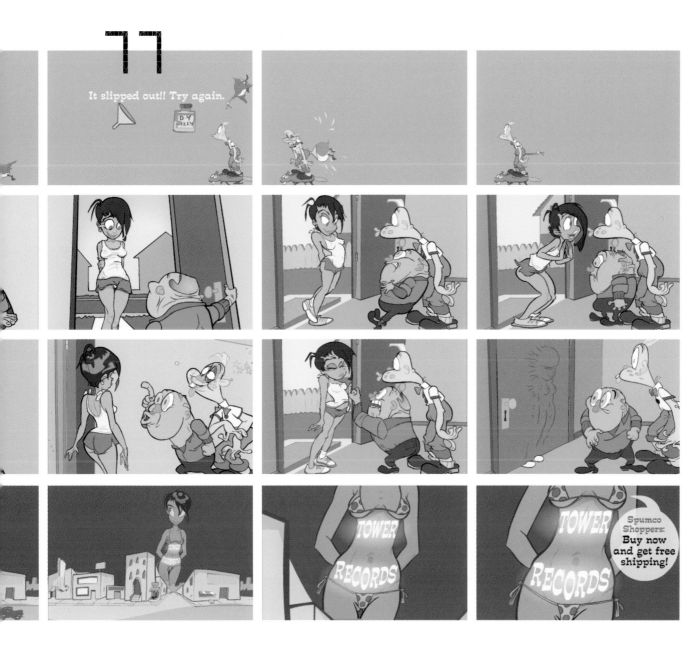

What are your recommended websites?

//seg.com/ufc/index.html
www.raymondscott.com/index.htm
www.liberace.org/museum.html
www.chick.com/catalog/tractlist.asp
www.qis.net/~minidonk/donktext.htm

What single thing would most improve the web from a creative/design point of view?

The technology for doing animation on the web is pretty primitive right now. But the biggest problem is one of standardization of technology. It is difficult to make a consistent presentation for all of the various platforms and browsers out there. The difficulty involved in downloading and installing multimedia plug-ins is a big drawback too. In general, the web should be more consistent and simpler for the viewers to use. However, the most important thing about the web is that content is king. No amount of flashy design can cover up for a site that has nothing to offer.

What is the future of the website in terms of design?

We plan to incorporate more interactivity in our web cartoons. We are also working on simple interactive comic stories that don't require a plug-in to view.

What will be the next big design trend in websites?

I think that many websites have become very complicated and difficult to navigate. Links are described by vague words meant to intrigue, but all they do is annoy. People know what they want to see. They don't want to click on a link without knowing where it leads. Simple, straightforward site navigation is the key to moving people through a site. If you make it difficult by putting a million unclear links on a single page, they pop off to someone else's web page.

EDEN

address	www.eden.sigma6.com
concept	Eden is an online comic set in some distant, post-apocalyptic future. Its familiar-sounding tale of charismatic outcasts fighting against an oppressive regime is enlivened by the interactive experience. Users can find out more about the cast, key locations and concepts via a pop-up Shockwave window, and choose a soundtrack. 'Conceptually and artistically, the site is intended to function as a part of the story itself – it is an artefact, a communications/control tool of a sinister New World Order that has literally been hacked into by the technologically adept children of the story's post-apocalyptic age,' says Jani Anderson, creative director of Sigma6, the site's co-creator.
credits	Creator and illustrator: Kenjji Marshall Co-creator: Jani Anderson Lead developer (Flash and sound effects): Jennifer Dugan Writer/editor: Matt Mullins HTML and soundtrack: Dale Lawrence
software	Soundforge, Flash, Photoshop, Streamline

CARTOON NETWORK

EDEN

81

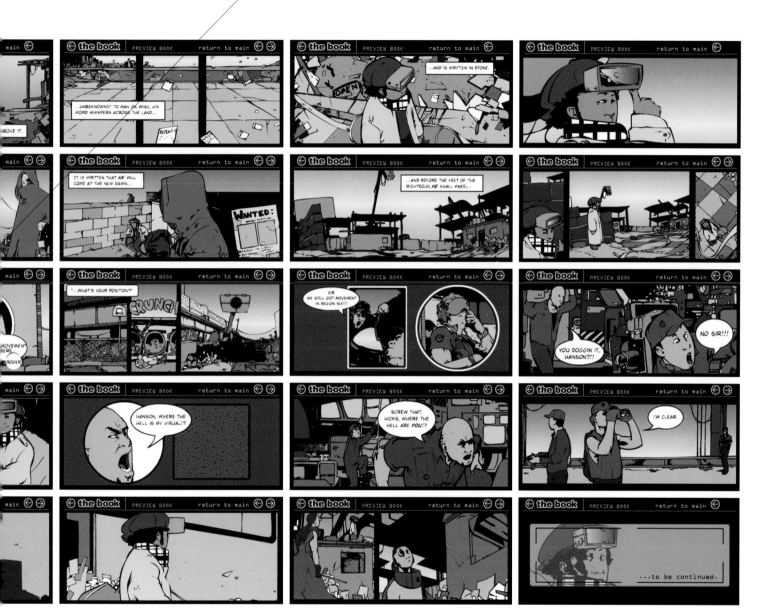

MOVIEMAKER

address	www.dfilm.com/new_site/movie_index.html
concept	The Digital Film Festival's Moviemaker game allows anyone to make their own Java movie. The user chooses how many characters they want (one or two – it's not exactly *Ben Hur*), what type of film they'd like, the cast, what kind of sky and what kind of background. They can then preview the movie before e-mailing it to friends.
credits	Creative director: Ardith Rigby Programmer: Ben Rigby of Akimbo Design
software	Photoshop, Homesite, Dreamweaver, Flash, Flash Generator

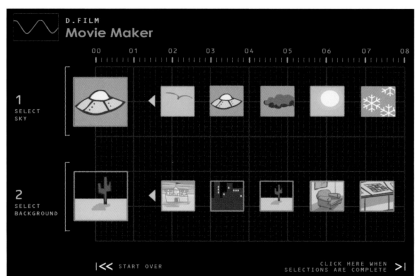

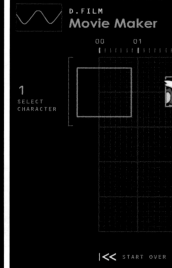

Ben Rigby

↖ Akimbo Design

CARTOON NETWORK

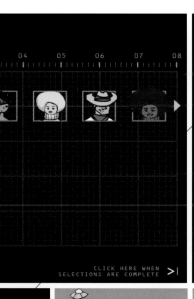

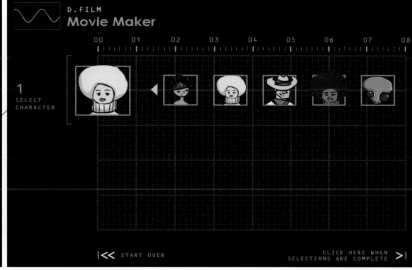

What are your recommended websites?

www.yahoo.co.uk
www.atlas.com
www.volumeone.com
//developer.netscape.com/docs/manuals/communicator/jsguide4/index.htm
www.fuse98.com

What single thing would most improve the web from a creative/design point of view?

More bandwidth!

What is the future of the website in terms of design?

I feel that web, television and film will eventually collide into a hybrid thing that is like interactive moving pictures. Users will be able to watch full-frame video, buy a product that they see within the video, talk to friends and play an interactive game all on the same machine at the same time. Design-wise, this means that design firms will also have to become web-savvy film production houses which is the direction that Akimbo Design is headed.

What will be the next big design trend in websites?

As far as trends go, it seems that they are mostly driven by the technology. The 5.0 browsers will allow us to make increasingly dynamic sites. For example, we'll be able to lay out the page based on current browser size, processor speed and screen resolution.

ATOMICTV

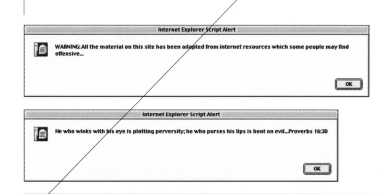

CARTOON NETWORK

address	www.cartoonnetwork.com
concept	The CartoonNetwork is the place for cartoon fans to go on the net. Sections of the site include the Department of Cartoons (D.O.C.) which is all about what goes into the making of cartoons, and features video clips, storyboards, background art, model sheets and episode designs from a wide variety of cartoons. This is content that has never been seen before. Another section, Favourites, is about cartoon fans' favourite characters and features trivia and video clips. Space Ghost News is a parody of a CNN-style news site. Space Ghost and his pals continually misinterpret the earth news and give their skewed take on it. This is a true news site which is updated daily. The Games section is a blend of online and downloadable games, icons and screensavers. Many of the games have been created in Shockwave and are playable online. Network H.Q. is the centre for information about the network and on-air programming. Finally, in Web Premier Toons, which is soon to be launched, new, interactive cartoons will be premiered on the web.
credits	Designers: Peter Girardi, Chris Capuozzo and Matthew Canton Programmers: Fred Kahl, Nina Ong and Erik Voigt
software	Illustrator, Photoshop, GoLive Cyberstudio, Flash, Director

CARTOON NETWORK

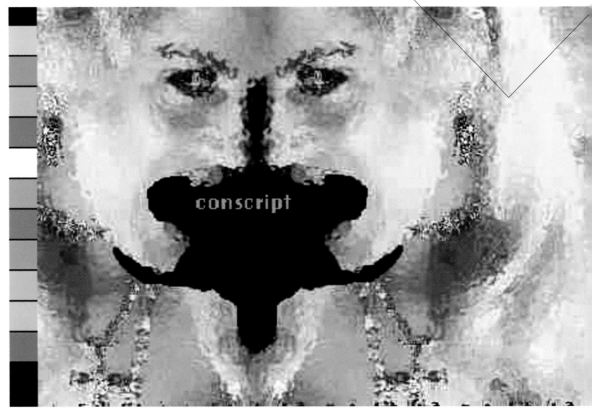

ATOMICTV

David Bickerstaff

← www.atomictv.com

address	www.atomictv.com
concept	Atomictv was established in 1997 by artist and designer David Bickerstaff. The site is a creative platform for the interactive and multimedia works he develops in collaboration with programmers and other artists. 'A person entering the space of atomictv is relieved of their usual determinates. They become no more than what they do or experience in the role of passenger, customer, voyeur or browser. Atomictv ponders the basic notion that computers lead to a solitary exercise in social life and perpetuates the contemporary paradox: one can be alone and at the same time in communication with everybody else around the world.'
credits	Concept: David Bickerstaff Design and images: David Bickerstaff and Paul Whittington Programming: David Bickerstaff, Paul Whittington and Andi Freeman Sound: David Bickerstaff and Julian Bromley
software	Dreamweaver, Director, Photoshop, Freehand, BBEdit, GifBuilder

And if your eye causes you to sin, pluck it out. It is better for you to enter the kingdom of God with one eye than to have two eyes and be thrown to hell...Mark 9:47

87

OK

Internet Explorer Script Alert

From the fruit of his lips a man is filled with good things as surley as the work of his hands rewards him...Proverbs 12:14

OK

Internet Explorer Script Alert

Whoever loves discipline loves knowlege, but he who hates correction is stupid...Proverbs 12:1

OK

Internet Explorer Script Alert

On the contrary, those parts of body that seems to be weaker are indispensable, and the parts that we think are less honourable we treat with special honour. And the parts that are unpresentable are treated with special modesty...1 Corinthians 12:22-23

OK

What are your recommended websites?

www.thewoodcutter.com/sneakpreview/
intro.htm
www.day-dream.com
www.absurd.org
www.dhky.com
www.fresh55.com

What single thing would most improve the web from a creative/design point of view?

Development of a single browser product that offers consistency in appearance and performance for your website across platforms, has a more aesthetically considered interface, and improved sophistication for reproducing type.

What is the future of the website in terms of design?

A movement towards more television-style multimedia environments that reflect the development of improved compression technology.

What will be the next big design trend in websites?

Probably experimentation with dynamic HTML.

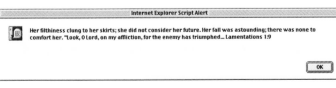

Internet Explorer Script Alert

Her filthiness clung to her skirts; she did not consider her future. Her fall was astounding; there was none to comfort her. "Look, O Lord, on my affliction, for the enemy has triumphed... Lamentations 1:9

OK

Internet Explorer Script Alert

Like a gold ring in a pig's snout is a beautiful woman who shows no discretion...Proverbs 11:22

OK

CARTOON NETWORK

Lee Misenheimer

↙ www.destroyrockcity.com

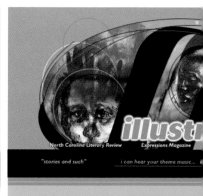

DESTROY ROCK CITY

address	www.destroyrockcity.com
concept	Despite the texture and depth offered by hand-drawn illustration, it is still somewhat of a rarity online. Lee Misenheimer's webzine Destroy Rockcity is a great example of what can be achieved using a combination of old and new media. 'Destroy Rockcity originated as a comic zine featuring my own work, distributed for free at local punk rock shows. It just kind of migrated to the web, with a little more emphasis on integrating graphic elements into the illustration. Essentially the site deals with strange characters who brandish odd tools or objects.'
credits	Lee Misenheimer
software	Photoshop, Illustrator, GifBuilder, Flash

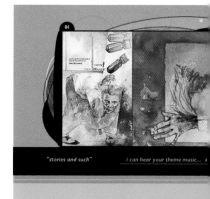

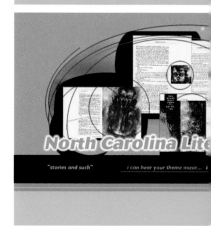

What are your recommended websites?

www.volumeone.com
www.mach5design.com
www.shift.jp.org
www.eboy.com
www.netbaby.se

What single thing would most improve the web from a creative/design point of view?

Speed. It's hard to restrain myself when it comes to large, juicy graphics. Luckily, Flash is there to add some dynamic flavor at lower speeds. I would really love to inject a nice, crazy After Effects project into my site though.

What is the future of the website in terms of design?

Flash should really play an important role, as well as re-emphasis on storytelling (longer stories and more developed characters).

What will be the next big design trend in websites?

Everything is getting pretty cute. Small, iconic bitmap characters will rule.

FIXED PRICE LOCAL CALLS

CREATION RECORDS

address	www.creation.co.uk

concept

Alan McGee's Creation was one of the first record labels to respond to the challenge/threat posed by the internet in a positive way. The homepage consists of a number of line drawings of appropriate objects: a camera for the link to the webcam, a guitar for the Oasis page. These are annotated with symbols reminiscent of those found on the periodic table and which bear the initials of the subject they link to. As the information needs to be updated almost daily, an editing program was developed by Kleber so the client could do it themselves. In addition to the interactive interface there is a pull-down menu for quick access to its various sections for regular users, or those who simply can't be bothered with the concept of interaction through play.

credits

Interface design, generic graphic design: Draught (David Gibson and Michael Lenz)
Illustration and animation: Joe Berger
Programming design: Kleber (Chris McGrail and Dorian Moore)
Production and creativity: Muso (Kieran Evans and Andrew Pavord)

software

Director, Shockwave, Photoshop, Flash

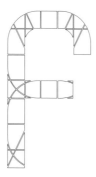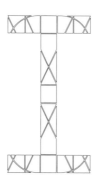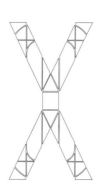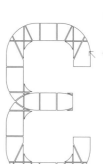

Michael Lenz

www.creation.co.uk

Andi Freeman

www.deepdisc.com

Creation Records

Quick Access Menu. ▼ Go

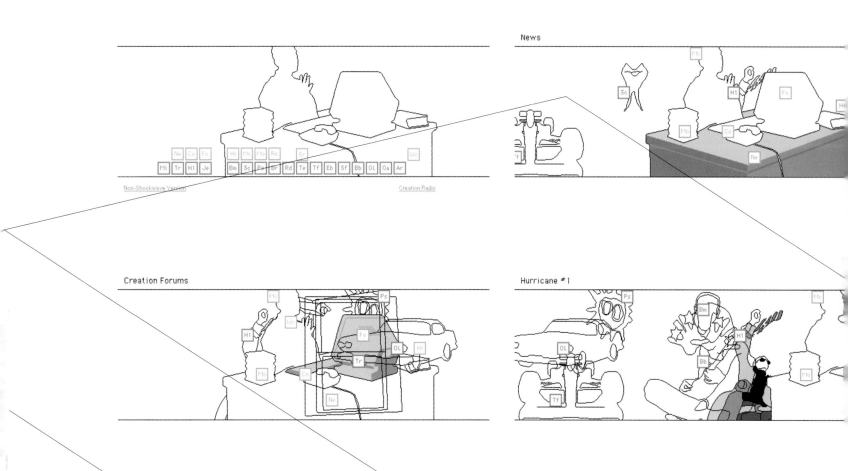

News

Non-Shockwave Version

Creation Radio

Creation Forums

Hurricane #1

What are your recommended websites?

www.resfest.com
www.grandroyal.com
www.shockrave.com
www.zelda64.com

What single thing would most improve the web from a creative/design point of view?

Obviously it needs to work faster and without the need to access and download plug-ins, i.e. Shockwave and Flash. An overriding people's choice of system font would be good too.

What is the future of the website in terms of design?

Generally, the design, and function, of websites will improve as the technology improves, giving designers more options. The problem at the moment is that most of the internet is ruled by programmers with a small bag of tricks and little visual design sense (this is similar to what happened to design with the introduction of PCs and desktop printers). I think eventually people will begin to see the difference as more good designers start working in collaboration with good programmers.

What are your recommended websites?

www.jodi.org
www.irational.org
www.nettime.org
www.nationwide-league.co.uk
www.bargainholidays.com

What single thing would most improve the web from a creative/design point of view?

Fixed-price local calls.

What is the future of the website in terms of design?

Better client targeting of multiple design schemes; more dynamic content and less choice; client side programming; less focus on 'sites' and more focus on content, products and issues.

REASONS for TEMPORARY LULLS IN PRODUCTIVE THINKING

 Boredom.

 Exhaustion.

L SHAPED ROOM.
I AM ASLEEP.
A WOMAN WRAPS ME IN BANDAGES.
THERE IS THE BIGGEST INSECT STINGY BASTARD I EVER SEEN IN THE OTHER SIDE OF THE ROOM.
WE ARE TOO SCARED TO KILL IT.
AND IT WILL NOT LEAVE.
well, anyway, i gotta go + liedown

not sleeping okay/drinking too much. trapped in hyperspace.?.the girl disappeared, smiling and blowing kisses. A white light flooded the room/this was the moment of awakening
relieved to find themselves in their own company...*someone (text unclear) did not awaken, this was a white nightmare: faces aglow with laughing, limp complacency/apparently*

perhaps it's inevitable.

perhaps one has to choose between nothing at all.

or impersonating what one is.

type 'apple A'
type 'apple C'
type 'apple V'
type 'apple X'
type 'apple Z'

And then do it again and again until it's time to go.

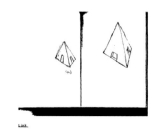

Link

dani.so

what a clean city
im kinda sleep ee
call an ambulance
i feel icky

invasion
of bodily fluids

must learn to floss

no substitute for a healthy smile

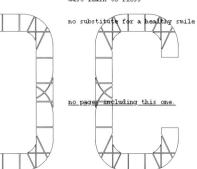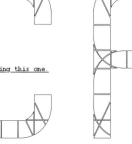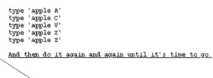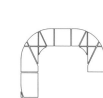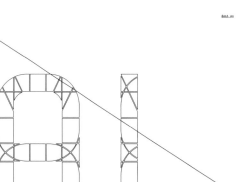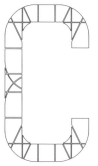

no pages including this one.

advice for robots

if you feel that/low again.
please try. remain
inside/circleof
friends./see next instruction

softness
shaking
all in its right being

it willpass
onlypart/not last

saltwater good for cleaning

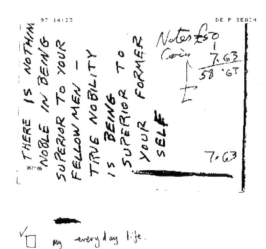

ce were

RADIOHEAD

address	www.radiohead.com
concept	A formula for representing rock and pop bands on the net has developed which comprises information on upcoming releases, tour schedules, video clips, sound files and perhaps some kind of live discussion with band members. Radiohead's site rejects all this. Stanley Donwood, the British designer behind Radiohead's sleeve art and one of the creators of the site, describes it as providing accommodation 'for sketches and ideas and images that don't fit in anywhere'. 'It is very hard to navigate around and has no funky animations or downloadable music or videoclips,' he explains. 'It has no news, no gig guide; no useful information at all. There are a lot of unofficial Radiohead sites that do all the things we don't. We link to them because they're useful and we aren't.' Instead, this official site for the band consists of abstract lines of type that lead on from one another when clicked and which are occasionally combined with equally abstract sketches, snatches of lyrics and elements of sleeve art.
credits	Design and programming: Stanley Donwood and Doctor Tchock and Matt Bale
software	Simpletext

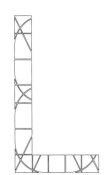

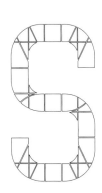

ANDI FREEMAN → 93

HOME SWEET HOME

BREAKING & ENTERING

PREPARATION
WHAT TO WEAR
BEING DISCREET
MAKING AN ENTRANCE
CODE BREAKING
EDUCATION

...through the front door. We talked to six uninvited guests to find out how they do it.

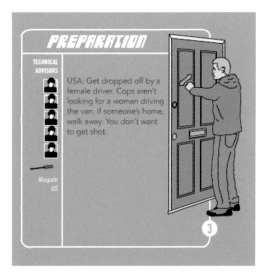

PREPARATION

TECHNICAL ADVISORS

USA: Get dropped off by a female driver. Cops aren't looking for a woman driving the van. If someone's home, walk away. You don't want to get shot.

Margate
US

3

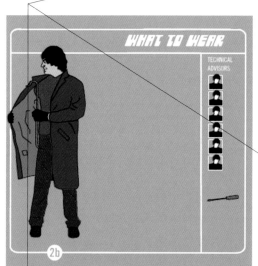

WHAT TO WEAR

TECHNICAL ADVISORS

2b

BEING D

TECHNICAL ADVISORS

PREPARATION

TECHNICAL ADVISORS

4

WHAT TO WEAR

TECHNICAL ADVISORS

2a

BEING DISCRE

TECHNICAL ADVISORS

COLORS

address	www.benetton.com/colors
concept	Online versions of print magazines vary enormously in quality. One of the best is this version of Benetton's themed magazine, *Colors*. On the web, *Colors* is a buzzy, lively experience making extensive use of Shockwave. Back issues can be accessed by clicking on the issue numbers displayed along the bottom. The current issue dominates the main space, revealing its content via a typographic interface of terms relevant to the central theme of the issue. Click on a word and a pop-up Shockwave window carries editorial consisting of graphics, sound, photography and animation. Online content has been tailored to suit the medium with less reliance on photography than the printed version (perhaps they had problems clearing rights) and more illustration, graphics and typography. 'Ultimately,' says project director Tom Hobbs, 'the website tries to do what the magazine can't.'
credits	Design, interface and programming: New Media@Fabrica Editorial director: Oliviero Toscani Project direction: Tom Hobbs Designers – 'Fabricantes': Lillian Coryn (Toys 29–Heart 30); Adam Schroeder (Toys 29–Heart 30); Steve Bowden (Smoking 21–Touch 28); Lloyd Thomas (Smoking 21–Home 27); Spencer Higgins (Smoking 21–Time 26) Guest contributors: Jen Dugan (Hearts 30); George LaRou (Toys 29); Matt Owens (Touch 28)
software	Photoshop, Illustrator, ImageReady, Director, Flash, Dreamweaver, SoundEdit, Freehand, BBEdit

snapshots.
sentient beings/cold(soothing)
dont.
go.
will only want to come back.

not just circle
not just being
(our radiance/andmeaning.)
sorry that didnt write(be there)
when you wanted(be there)
now writing
now saying

please remember all the good things

now
File/Print.../Print(on my wall stuck for remembering)message ends

What does it mean to be
Blind & Deaf  ?

Lucia d'Ugo, 60, lives in Osimo, Italy. She uses speech and the Italian manual alphabet to communicate (we asked the questions in Malossi, she replied in Italian) There are several manual alphabets in the world. To translate these questions into the one used in your country, see page 98 of the magazine.

COLORS

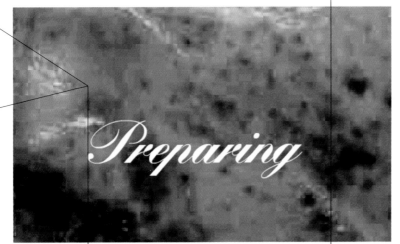

Preparing

⊙ the ideal body   ⊙ how fat is your world?   ⊙ eat fat   ⊙ false needs   ⊙ Adam W. tastes the news   **COLORS** 25

Most bottled water is packaged in plastic. In the USA alone people empty 2

31 WATER

fat

three hundred million people

all with the same face

everything i say/do is

take me and you'll ge

there

⊙ the ideal body   ⊙ how fat is your world?   ⊙ eat fat   ⊙ false needs   ⊙ Adam W. tastes the news   **COLORS** 25

CHOOSE A STORY

numbers mean nothing

god blessed you with a pretty face

right school

right parents

Tom Hobbs

← 96-98 Fabrica

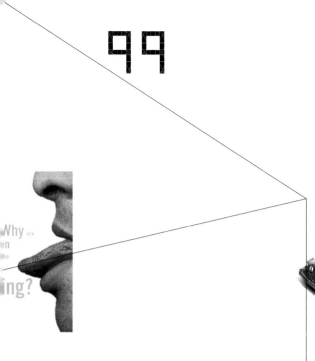

Why are
en
the
ing?

Daimler-Benz Land

Population: Like most rich countries, Multinational Land offers only restricted entry. The world's 200 richest companies operate in hundreds of countries and control a quarter of the planet's economy, but provide work for less than 0.01 percent of the world's population.

Economy: Daimler-Benz citizens have a secure income: The automobile company—which inspired the Zimbabwean Mercedes shown here—ranks as number 51 among the world's top 200 economies (just above IBM and Malaysia), while the aerospace division—which makes land mines, jet planes and missiles—is number 13 among the top 100 defense manufacturers.

Prospects: It pays to live in Multinational Land. While one-fifth of the world's population went to sleep hungry last night, sales of Daimler-Benz's luxury cars were up 110 percent last year. The land mine industry does its bit to keep Daimler-Benz afloat, thanks to the company's two-pronged approach: One branch makes the land mines, and another can be hired to clean them up.

Caterpillar Land

Population: Caterpillar Land is relatively small (full-time population 65,947), but it supplies most of the world's earthmoving equipment (including wheel loaders like this toy version from Zil Land).

Allies: Plenty. In 1995, the world had 40,000 multinational corporations. In 1995, there were 40,000. Ninety percent of the largest northern industrialized countries; more than half are from Japan, Germany, the Netherlands, Britain and the USA.

Daily Life: Multinational companies control most of the world's oil, gasoline, diesel and jet fuel and minerals. They manufacture and sell most of the world's cars, airplanes, communications satellites, computers, home electronics, chemicals, medicines and biotechnology products. They harvest most of the world's wood and make most of its paper. They control the world's seed (growing 90 percent of export crops like tobacco, cotton and bananas, and own most of the planet's genetic seed banks). They own 90 percent of the world's technology and product patents. They emit 50 percent of the world's greenhouse gases. In Multinational Land, you always have something to do.

tic bottles an hour.

Losing interest is the first step

on a slippery slope. Prolonged boredom can lea

Queue shape is vital,

is vital, report the experts at Walt Disney Imagin

What are your recommended websites?

www.amaze.co.uk/noodlebox
www.volumeone.com
www.mediaboy.com
www.eden.sigma6.com
www.d-film.com

What single thing would most improve the web from a creative/design point of view?

To see more people using the medium for its strengths, not what could be felt as its weaknesses. There seems to be an emphasis on mediums that can only be influences and informers, i.e. print and television. The web is very young, and whilst video game technology still has a big part to play, there has to be a fear that it is moving in a very linear direction,

What is the future of the website in terms of design?

The actual graphic style of Colors follows the print magazine closely. By this I mean general fonts usage, colour and feel. But this is just a formality. The main experimentation will continue to be with its interface, how the user (visitor) actually accesses the content. But in addition, how they actually respond to it. The magazine is meant to provoke discussion

What will be the next big design trend in websites?

It could be one of a number of things. Probably the video industry, as bandwidth allows, will change the face of the web. As will DVD for sure; cable modems are already a reality (as is interactive television), and with an already highly developed cable infrastructure, the web could be a very different place in a few years.

WORD

address	www.word.com
concept	This is a magazine site that combines visuals, sound, motion and text. The content is designed to be experiential in nature, consisting largely of first-person stories and autobiographical essays about the lives of ordinary people. These articles are supplemented by an eclectic array of visual art, photography, underground comics, animation, video, music, games and online conversation. The *New York Times* described Word as 'a kind of hip, lo-fi New Yorker magazine for a new generation'.
credits	Art director: Yoshi Sodeoka Technology director: Ranjit Bhatnagar Senior designer: Jason Mohr Designer: Jason Huang Production: Frank Roldan
software	Photoshop, Illustrator, ImageReady, Premiere, AfterEffects, Director, Freehand, Flash, Dreamweaver, SoundEdit, BBEdit, Infini-D, Soundforge

Yoshi Sodeoka

← www.word.com

What are your recommended websites?

www.day-dream.com
www.e13.com
www.hotwired.co.jp
www.leisuretown.com

What single thing would most improve the web from a creative/design point of view?

Browsers with intuitive interface design that don't crash.

What is the future of the website in terms of design?

The website is a temporary phase in interactive media. Sooner or later, it will be replaced by something that is faster, better looking and easier to use – or several somethings, as different needs and uses of the internet evolve. These new incarnations might be viewed with handheld devices or VR goggles; they might look like 3D game worlds or abstract paintings, or they might look like something nobody has thought of yet.

What will be the next big design trend in websites?

Right now, many designers are making their websites simpler because of the demand for quick, easy information. But in the next few years, as bandwidth and time spent online continue to increase, users will be looking for satisfying experiences – entertainment and meaningful content. That will lead to more richly designed websites that take advantage of high-bandwidth multimedia but remain easy to use underneath. The smartest designers will start figuring out ways to deliver a customized experience that matches the demands and needs of the user.

jellydogs jellied eels

we go to a restaurant there is meat in the bread there is not enough seats for everyone there is meat in everything jellylikefat pink slices pink/climbing up

photos are falling down.

Link. Link. Link. Link. Link. Link.

Ben Benjamin

www.superbad.com

WORD

i swallow glass
a dream palace in the sun for stressed out executives
there are spies
pinhole cameras in every room

everybody wants a piece of windowpane
everybody wants a piece of broken glass
everybody wants a shattered piece of the windows/splinters
to show their friends
to take home with them
and watch the light turning into windows

a strange mistake to make
turn the other cheek
the sirens in the sea
i
swallow glass

with the majority of sites still being very much broadcast. There is little that truly exploits the web's ability to use interactive possibility, hyper-linearity and the possibility of creating user-driven environments (Colors perhaps included in this). We need to find a visual language that has this in mind – dynamic graphics and other content and design that responds to usage. And not just on an individual 'client' level but actually affecting the site as a whole (for other visitors).

– the website does not at present exploit this. This could mean dynamic content, maybe that which the user constructs out of predetermined graphics and content (Flash Generator or Director technology allows this, like Digital Film [d-film.com] has experimented with). Colors could be a great discussion and research resource; it would be interesting to experiment with this purely as visual design.

What are your recommended websites?

www.redsmoke.com
www.iscient.com.au/~lil
www.e13.com
www.dhky.com
www.deluxoland.com

What single thing would most improve the web from a creative/design point of view?

I thought the web was going to be everyone's opportunity to make and present their own art and ideas. As it's turned out, checking out the web makes it seem like everyone just wants to sell things. I don't necessarily think that the marketing aspect of the web makes it bad, but the web would be more interesting if people were more inclined to create than to sell things.

Also: higher resolution monitors.

What is the future of the website in terms of design?

It looks like the browser-makers are giving designers more and more control over how their pages look, which is mostly good, because then design for the web will continue to improve. The downside is that as websites get more complicated, it will require more money, time and organization to create professional-looking sites; a likely result will eventually be a more marked difference between corporate sites and personal sites.

What will be the next big design trend in websites?

It will probably be whatever the next big software feature makes it easy to do. (Like the blurred Photoshop dropshadow a few years ago. Or the way people started doing a lot of animation after Flash came out.) Hopefully, though, sites will start to simplify and clarify.

Erik Spiekermann,
MetaDesign

↙ www.audi-tt.com

↘ Dominic James

www.deep.co.uk

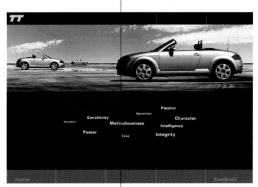

AUDI-TT

address	www.audi-tt.com
concept	The attention to detail that the German car-maker Audi puts into its vehicles is reflected in MetaDesign's site for the sporty TT model. This 'web event' was an integral part of the launch marketing campaign rather than just an afterthought. Making full use of Dynamic HTML it proves that cutting-edge innovation is possible even for such a heavyweight client. Audi's head of design discusses the vision behind the project on video and can also be called on to comment about a particular feature of the car in the Design section. Various shots of the car are combined with quotes from and pictures of other members of the design team. Users can download a commercial and screensaver as well as being able to find out when the car will be launched in their part of the world.
credits	Design: Alexander Baumgardt, Thomas Noller, Daniel Jenett and Vicky Tiegelkamp at MetaDesign
software	DHTML. Plug-ins: Real-Video and Quicktime

What are your recommended websites?

www.cnet.com
www.audi.de
www.typospace.de
www.suction.com
www.fedex.com

What single thing would most improve the web from a creative/design point of view?

A unified DOM.

What is the future of the website in terms of design?

Simplification.

What will be the next big design trend in websites?

Vector graphics embedded into HTML.

What are your recommended websites?

www.macnn.com
www.nma.co.uk
www.thinkmap.com
www.apple.com
www.railtrack.co.uk

What single thing would most improve the web from a creative/design point of view?

WYSIWYG – What You See Is What You Get – This would have to be what every designer would want from the internet, for example, being able to choose a typeface or colour and know that ALL your viewers would see the page the same way that you designed it.

What is the future of the website in terms of design?

The ability to create a fully enabled multimedia environment, that is personalized or specialized to your viewer, and that you as a designer can create without relying on others to provide the glue. I suppose you could say... DTW... DeskTopWebber.

What will be the next big design trend in websites?

Using Flash to create beautiful, interactive websites.

ROADRUNNER

address	www.roadrunner.co.uk
concept	Retail businesses on the web are represented by both full-scale e-commerce sites allowing for online purchasing, and sites which seek to drive custom to a real shop. Roadrunner is a neat example of the latter. It details rollerblading, skateboarding and BMX products sold by the shop as well as related services and events. The PS:SP (PlayStation: Skate Park) area features Quicktime VR of the park and movies of it in use.
credits	Design and programming: Deep Creative
software	Cyberstudio, VRtools, Photoshop

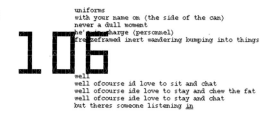

uniforms
with your name on (the side of the can)
never a dull moment
he's in charge (personnel)
freezeframed inert wandering bumping into things

well
well ofcourse id love to sit and chat
well ofcourse ide love to stay and chew the fat
well ofcourse ide love to stay and chat
but theres someone listening in

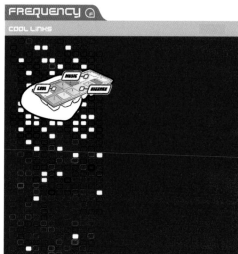

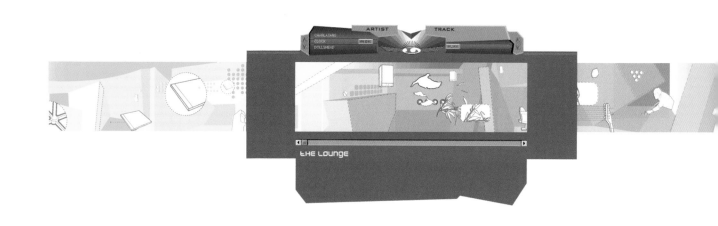

FREQUENCY

address	www.frequency.co.uk
concept	British record label Frequency has a diverse portfolio of artists. Instead of giving each band their own site, Frequency cleverly brings everyone together within one highly colourful interface. Guests can listen to all the label's latest releases in the Lounge area and information on gigs and live webcasts is also available.
credits	Design and programming: Digit – Digital Experiences Ltd
software	Director, Shockwave, Photoshop, Freehand, Fontographer, Premiere, BBEdit, Dreamweaver, Flash

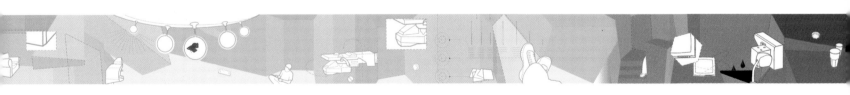

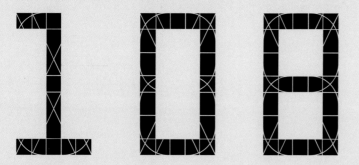

NOT JUST I.E.4

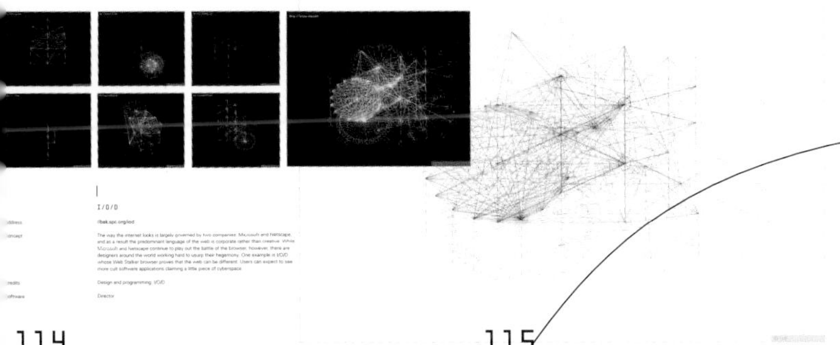

ICI LA LUNE

I/O/D

VISUAL THESAURUS

POST-HUMAN

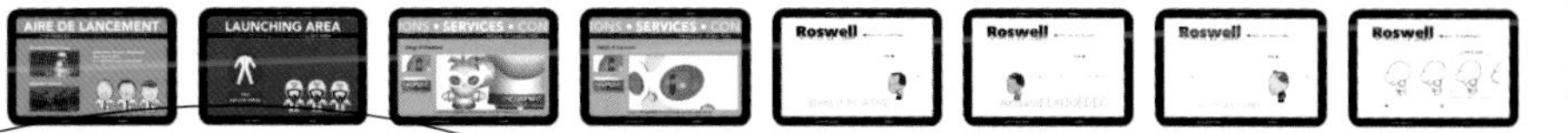

HUMAN   END

FLESH COM

What are your recommended websites?

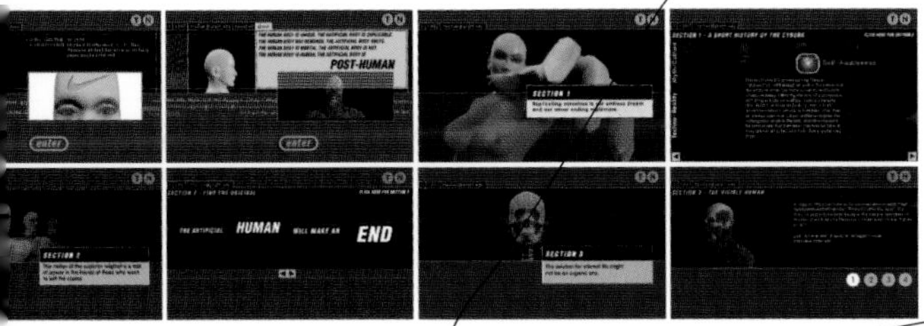

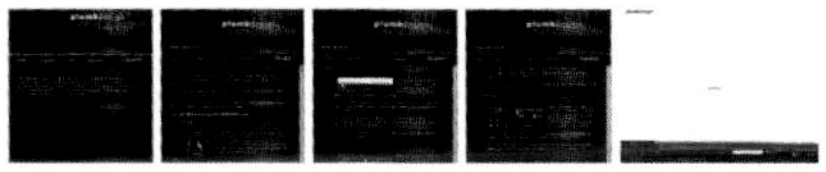

What single thing would most improve the web from a creative/design point of view?

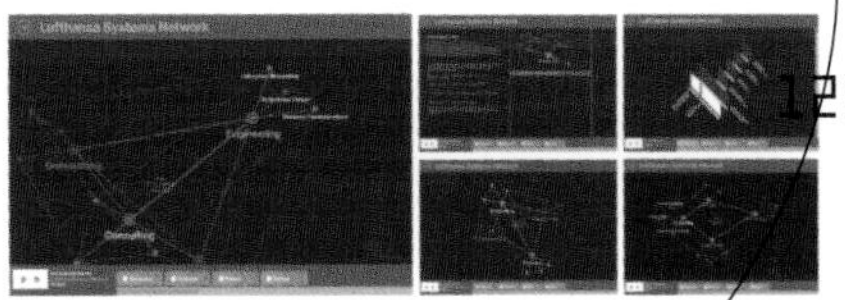

What is the future of the website in terms of design?

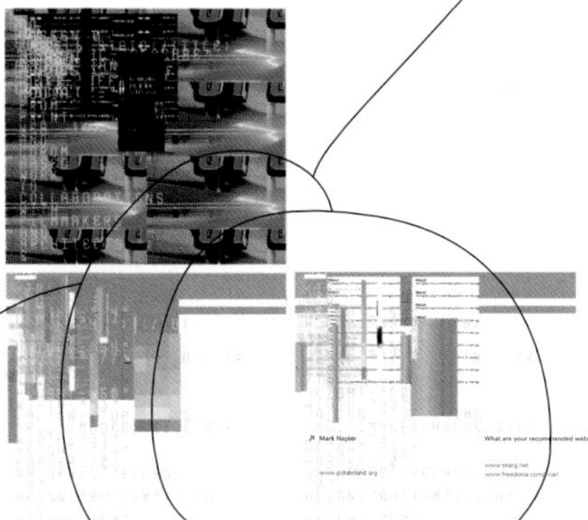

What will be the next big design trend in websites?

START!

FORK

www.fork.de

SHREDDER

POTATOLAND

www.potatoland.org

VISUALROUTE

www.visualroute.com

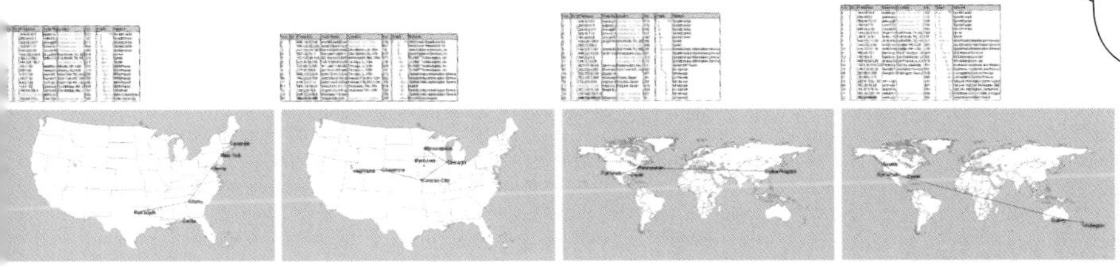

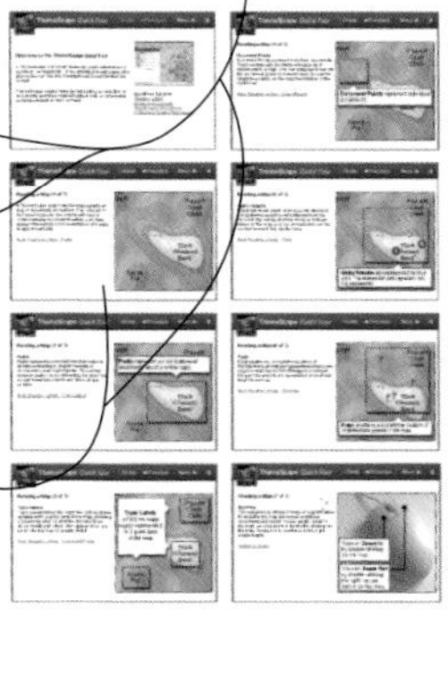

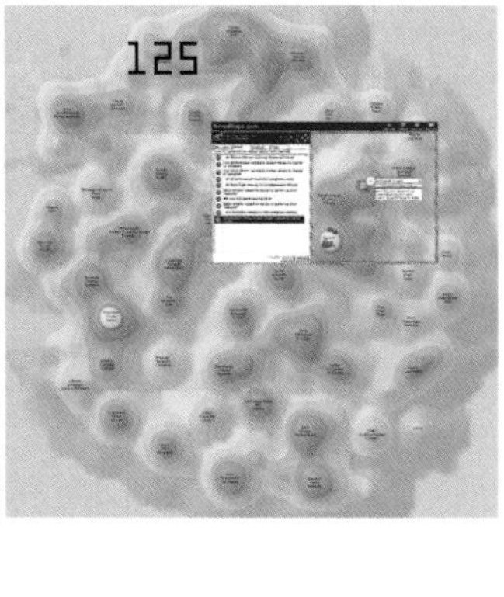

THEMESCAPE

www.cartia.com

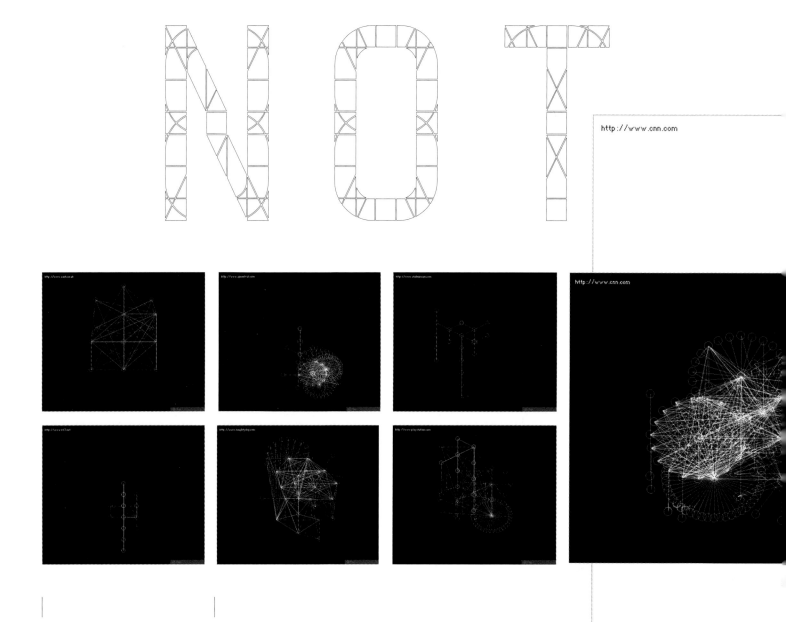

I/O/D

address	//bak.spc.org/iod
concept	The way the internet looks is largely governed by two companies: Microsoft and Netscape, and as a result the predominant language of the web is corporate rather than creative. While Microsoft and Netscape continue to play out the battle of the browser, there are designers around the world working hard to usurp their hegemony. One example is I/O/D whose Web Stalker browser proves that the web can be different. Users can expect to see more cult software applications claiming a little piece of cyberspace.
credits	Design and programming: I/O/D
software	Director

JUST

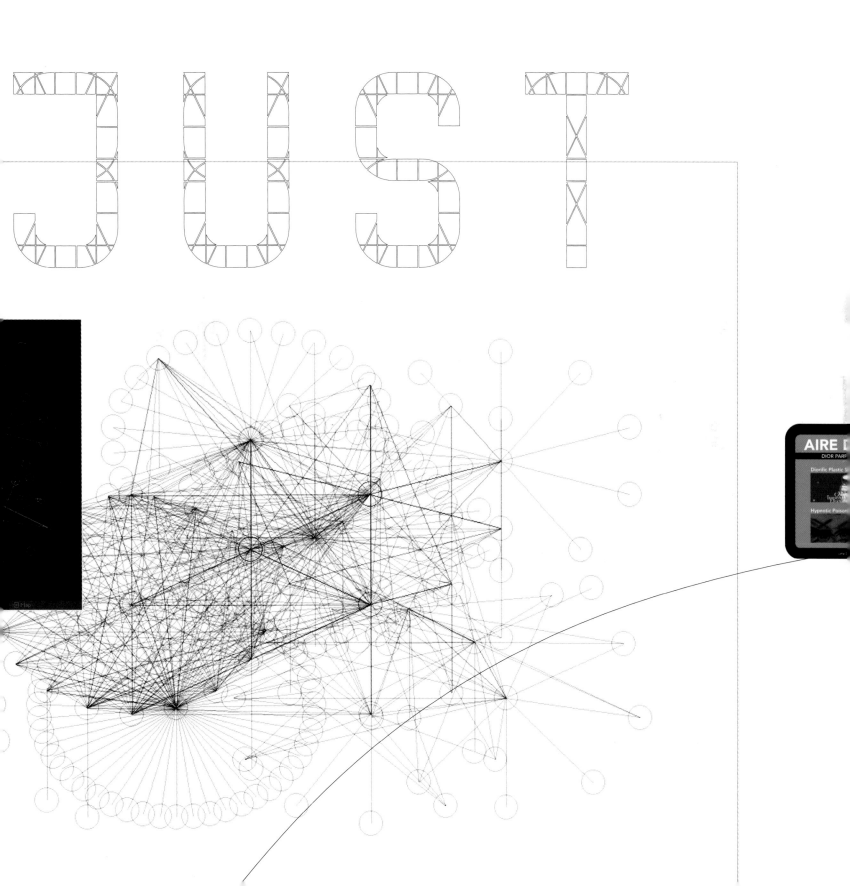

I.2.4

MARTIN DODGE → 13⁹

Benoit Platre

↗ www.icilalune.com

ICI LA LUNE

address	www.icilalune.com
concept	French design group Ici La Lune's research into interface design resulted in this site which they say explores a new navigation principle termed 'miniscrollfly'. 'The content follows the mouse. You navigate by going left or right. When you make a choice, you click and the content becomes a kind of section title,' explains designer Benoit Platre. The site is translated into three languages: French, English and Japanese, and makes innovative use of colour. Each language has its own colour and each subject heading its own hue. In addition, the site seeks to use Shockwave as more than just a means to run animations. The site 'is a Shockwave engine which calls different media from the server when needed,' says Platre. 'We wanted to be able to translate the website into CD-Rom format very easily: you can do it in about one hour.'
credits	Design: Arnaud Le Ouedec, Benoit Platre and Vincent Queguiner Music: Christophe Hamel and Charles Vannier Japanese translation: Aki Ikemura
software	Director, Flash, Photoshop, Illustrator, Dreamweaver

   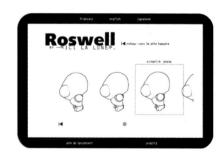

What are your recommended websites?

www.groovisions.com
www.amaze.co.uk/noodlebox
www.metadesign.de
www.heliozilla.com
www.audi-tt.com
(for the HTML design and the car!)

What single thing would most improve the web from a creative/design point of view?

The web needs innovations every day to give internet users the new kinds of emotions and sensations that these new media permit. The role of the designer is to imagine new products, new services and innovative design. The web designer has to understand two cultures: programming and graphics. It's the same as at the beginning of the twentieth century when industry permitted some very modern services which were designed as in the nineteenth century or before. There is the same reaction on the internet: the majority of websites are designed as A4 pages. The print thinking is still there. 'icilalune' tries to think in different ways.

What is the future of the website in terms of design?

The future of the website in terms of design lies in using and understanding new technologies which permit a real integration of contents, graphics and music, staged with a new kind of interactivity. The print spirit belongs to print; the internet and other new supports are still looking for their own culture and languages.

What will be the next big design trend in websites?

< scrolling=no > and Shockwave and/or Flash design.

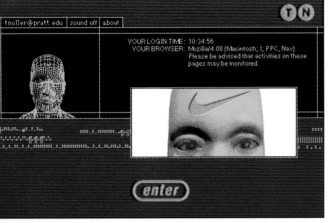

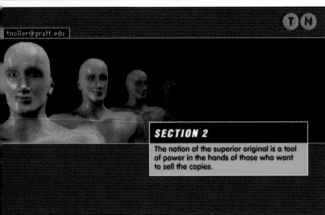

FLESH.COM

address	//acnet.pratt.edu/%7Etnoller/index.html
concept	Flesh.com is a site for 'loose reflections on the growing potential of artificial bodies and artificial intelligence,' says creator Thomas Noller. An explorative and immersive interface using the advantages of DHTML technology takes the user through the history of the cyborg and some possibilities for its future with an interactive timeline and 3D animations. 'I was trying to create an enticing, multi-dimensional environment with many texts, sounds and animations following the web's move towards a more story-telling approach rather than the random, arbitrary, hyper-link mess it used to be,' Noller says.
credits	Concept, design and programming: Thomas Noller
software	Photoshop, BBEdit, Fractal Design Poser

James Kuo

fresh55.com

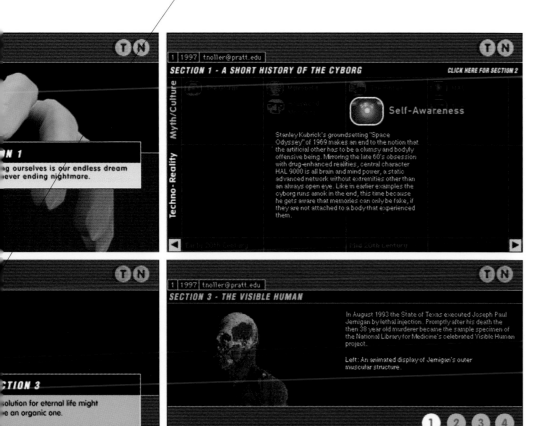

Myth/Culture | Techno-Reality

1 | 1997 | tnoller@pratt.edu

SECTION 1 - A SHORT HISTORY OF THE CYBORG

CLICK HERE FOR SECTION 2

Self-Awareness

Stanley Kubrick's groundsetting "Space Odyssey" of 1969 makes an end to the notion that the artificial other has to be a clumsy and bodyly offensive being. Mirroring the late 60's obsession with drug-enhanced realities, central character HAL 9000 is all brain and mind power, a static advanced network without extremities other than an always open eye. Like in earlier examples the cyborg runs amok in the end, this time because he gets aware that memories can only be fake, if they are not attached to a body that experienced them.

N 1

g ourselves is our endless dream
ever ending nightmare.

1 | 1997 | tnoller@pratt.edu

SECTION 3 - THE VISIBLE HUMAN

In August 1993 the State of Texas executed Joseph Paul Jernigan by lethal injection. Promptly after his death the then 38 year old murderer became the sample specimen of the National Library for Medicine's celebrated Visible Human project.

Left: An animated display of Jernigan's outer muscular structure.

CTION 3

solution for eternal life might
e an organic one.

What are your recommended websites?

www.ebay.com
www.amazon.com
www.cnn.com
www.altasmagzine.com
www.m-w.com
www.voyeurweb.com

What single thing would most improve the web from a creative/design point of view?

Providing viable content to the populous.
Opening the process back to the audience.
Delivering after the initial seduction.
Answering the 'that's nice, now what?'
question.

What is the future of the website in terms of design?

A new way of interaction after standardization.
A new way of delivering the message.
Moving away from kinetic eye-candy to the dynamic delivery of potent information.

What will be the next big design trend in websites?

Audience participation. Auto-generated data and information. Self-service content and a design to accommodate that. Resource capturing and virtual integrations between provider and user.

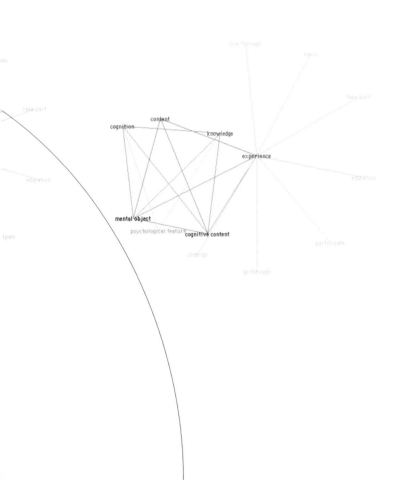

VISUAL THESAURUS

address	www.plumbdesign.com
	www.thinkmap.com

concept

An engaging experience in language and interface, the Plumb Design Visual Thesaurus is an artistic exploration that is also a learning tool. Through its dynamic interface, the Plumb Design Visual Thesaurus alters our relationship with language, creating poetry through user action, dynamic typography and design. Visitors to the site encounter a swirling nebula of words connected by a series of fine lines that represent sense relationships. Each click brings in more words from a connected database, creating a web of relationships that demonstrate linguistic associations and dependencies. Word forms that are more related become brighter and closer; those that are less related disappear from the display. The Thesaurus uses data from the WordNet database developed by the Cognitive Science Laboratory at a major university. This freely available database, first created in 1985 as a dictionary based on psycholinguistic theories, contains over 50,000 words and 40,000 phrases collected into more than 70,000 sense meanings. The word forms in the database are organized to approximate the manner in which we use and understand them.

credits

Concept development, software engineering and interface design: Marc Tinkler

software

The Thesaurus is built using Plumb Design's Thinkmap software which is written in Java

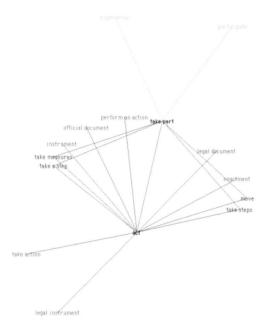
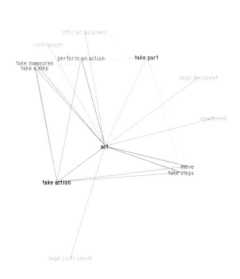

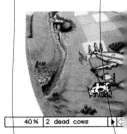

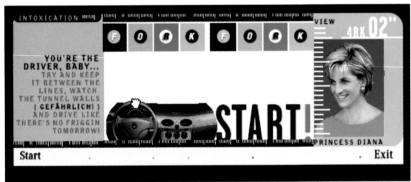

FORK

Manuel Funk

↗ www.fork.de

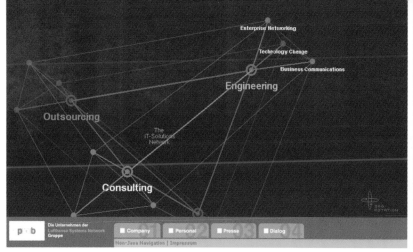

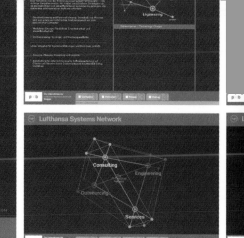

FORK

address

www.fork.de

concept

Fork are a German design group who manage to couple an aggressive, slick, modern style with a sick sense of humour. It is somewhat unusual for web designers to be commissioned to do the things they really like to do, but a glance at Fork's portfolio shows that their client work barely differs from their personal work. In 1997 Fork received a lot of press for their online game 'Diana Tunnel Racer'. They remain maladjusted, and in the games section of their site can be found titles such as 'Bosnia' and 'Cold War'. The best section, however, is Airbridge where users can view experimental interfaces, something that Fork excel at.

credits

Design: David Linderman
Games design and programming: Jeremy Abbett, Sascha Merg,
Andrea Mittmann, David Linderman
Project management: Manuel Funk
HTML programming: Nicole Kengyel
Java programming: Jan-Michael Stutt
Sound-design: Sascha Merg

software

BBEdit, Homesite, Fireworks, Flash, SoundEdit, Director

What are your recommended websites?

www.shift.jp.org
www.olympic.org
www.word.com
www.acne.se
www.popinger.com

What single thing would most improve the web from a creative/design point of view?

One of the most amazing interactive situations is that between a baby and its environment – no experience, lots of information. Creating a feeling of immersion with a healthy proportion of fun to frustration is the most important thing in exploring interactivity for the future.

What is the future of the website in terms of design?

Dynamic interfaces that demand immersion and prolong experiences. New metaphors for interface and content that drive 92 per cent of people mad, and leave the rest ecstatic.

What will be the next big design trend in websites?

Building new metaphors for the way we experience communication.

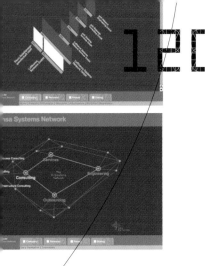

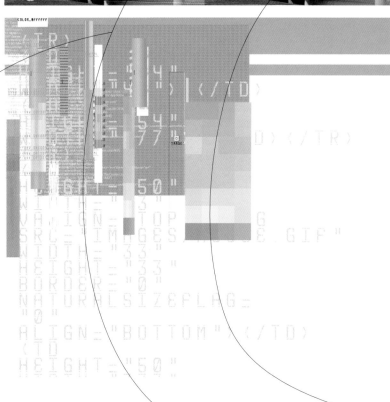

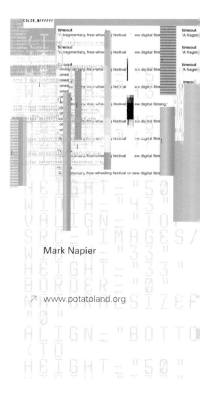

Mark Napier

www.potatoland.org

SHREDDER *1.0*

An alternative browsing experience brought to you by POTATOLAND.org and the Digital Landfill.
Type a URL into the textbox above and hit enter, or choose from one of these favorites.

About the *Shredder*

Copyright © 1998 Mark Napier. All rights reserved.

POTATOLAND

address	www.potatoland.org
concept	Mark Napier, the creator of Potatoland, is a man obsessed. His online creation is part gallery, part studio – some pieces are complete, some are just getting started. The site is always evolving, and the central theme of the artwork is evolving designs. 'Can an artwork be unpredictable, open-ended, not pre-determined?', asks Napier. 'Can artwork be the result of massive collaboration – with each visitor to the work in some way contributing to it? In this case, am I the artist? Or are the hundreds or thousands of visitors that contributed to the piece the real authors?' The network is an integral part of Napier's work and provides the raw material: traffic logs, multi-user systems, chat, database systems, data feeds, browsers. Highly recommended is the Shredder, Napier's rage against designers who use the internet like print. Napier says that the browser is an 'organ of perception through which we view the web'. The Shredder presents this global information as chaotic and irrational. By altering the HTML code before the browser sees it, the Shredder appropriates the data of the web, transforming it into abstraction, 'content becomes abstraction, text becomes graphics and information becomes art'.
credits	Design and programming: Mark Napier
software	Notepad, Photoshop, Perl (for server-side scripts), Borland JBuilder (for Java applets)

What are your recommended websites?

www.snarg.net
www.freedonia.com/~carl

What single thing would most improve the web from a creative/design point of view?

The web is perfect as it is. I'm very serious about this. I can't imagine an environment more filled with creative potential. The biggest challenge for me is just keeping up with all the possible uses of this medium. There are technology issues that I'd love to see fixed, browser incompatibilities and so on, but to me that's part of the challenge of the medium. I don't think of improving it so much as using it.

What is the future of the website in terms of design?

My design revolves around intensive user interaction. I present projects as clearly and simply as possible, taking my inspiration from software design. The site is an interface with a very specific function: to provide access to a wide variety of web artwork. As computers become more powerful, and (hopefully) browsers become more stable, I would like to make the site much more sensitive to the user interaction, to the point that it becomes a multi-user environment, where the visitors are connected together through the site. At the moment many of the projects at Potatoland are very memory intensive, and the average computer has trouble keeping up, so the current design is by necessity fairly spare. I'd like to create much richer navigation elements, perhaps incorporating visitor movement through the site into some of the artwork. But this requires the technology to become more stable and standardized.

What will be the next big design trend in websites?

Overall I don't see any clear cut winning trends coming soon. There's a lot of technology out there, and new standards are being developed all the time. It takes time to integrate all these technologies into some sort of workable whole. For example, Flash encompasses much of the functionality of HTML and Javascript, and Javascript is growing to include much of the functionality of Flash and other software development environments. Add to the mix all the audio plug-ins, various video formats (and then there's still Java lurking about), and you've got a stew of potential, without much clear structure. Now we're entering the delicate phase of finding how these pieces best fit together. The next trend is to sort the stew into something clear.

			CLIPS:
BODYCOUNT::	-1364		3
AMMO::	19		

			CLIPS:
BODYCOUNT::	0		3
AMMO::	80		

FORK

Hop	Err	IP Address	Node Na	Location	ms	Graph	Network
1		204.49.53.8	lightning.	Destin, FL 32541	122		Sprint/Centel
2		204.49.53.1	gateway.	Destin, FL 32541	147		Sprint/Centel
3		204.49.13.17	ans-gulfr	Tallahassee, FL 3	117		Sprint/Centel
4		204.49.7.17	cisco2-t	Tallahassee, FL 3	144		Sprint/Centel
5		199.44.9.35	cisco8-f5	Tallahassee, FL 3	200		Sprint/Centel
6		144.228.134.9	sl-gw10-f	Fort Worth, TX, US	214		Sprint
7		208.12.128.1	sl-fw-1-F	Fort Worth, TX, US	219		Sprint
8		144.228.180.2		Herndon, VA 2207	217		Sprint
9		4.0.1.106	atlanta1-i	Atlanta, GA, USA	215		BBN Planet
10		4.0.1.86	vienna1-i	Vienna, VA, USA	215		BBN Planet
11		4.0.3.126	nyc4-br1	New York, NY, US	305		BBN Planet
12		4.0.2.162	nyc4-br2	New York, NY, US	270		BBN Planet
13		4.0.2.185	nyc1-br2	New York, NY, US	240		BBN Planet
14		4.0.1.122	cambridg	Cambridge, MA, U	244		BBN Planet
15	2	199.94.205.3	cambridg	Cambridge, MA, U	247		NEARnet
16	2	131.192.16.114	tufts.bbn		306		BBN Corporation
17	4	130.64.175.2	Tab-7507	Somerville, MA 02	350		Tufts University

Hop	Err	IP Address	Node Name	Location	ms	Graph	Network
1		199.120.82.68	nwidt68.nwidt.con	Remsen, IA 51050	134		West Iowa Telephone Co.
2		199.120.82.254	nwidt-ether1.nwid	Remsen, IA 51050	157		West Iowa Telephone Co.
3		167.142.53.105	ins-border4-seria	Des Moines, IA, USA	141		Iowa Network Services, Inc.
4		167.142.54.1	ins-core1-ether1-	Des Moines, IA, USA	157		Iowa Network Services, Inc.
5		157.130.96.145	901.hssi4-0.GW1	Minneapolis, MN, USA	173		UUNET Technologies, Inc.
6		137.39.59.193	135.ATM4-0-0.CR	Chicago, IL, USA	198		UUNET Technologies, Inc.
7		137.39.13.101	411.atm11-0-0.br	Chicago, IL, USA	223		UUNET Technologies, Inc.
8		137.39.250.6	gw14-chi-8-0.spri	Chicago, IL, USA	203		UUNET Technologies, Inc.
9		144.232.0.153	sl-bb10-chi-2-1.sp	Chicago, IL, USA	172		Sprint/United Information Service
10		144.232.8.118	sl-bb3-kc-5-0-0.sp	Kansas City, MO, USA	202		Sprint/United Information Service
11		144.232.2.14	sl-bb1-kc-0-0-0.sp	Kansas City, MO, USA	256		Sprint/United Information Service
12		144.228.10.82	sl-bb2-che-3-1-0.	Cheyenne, WY, USA	229		Sprint
13		144.224.10.5	sl-gw3-che-0-0.sp	Cheyenne, WY, USA	229		Sprint/United Information Service
14		144.232.138.6	sl-intserv-1-0.spri		215		Sprint/United Information Service
15		192.41.43.189	visualroute.com	Highland, UT 84003	255		Icon Developments

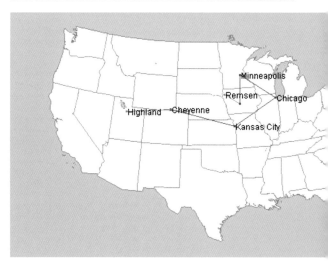

Jerry Jongerius

↗ Visualroute

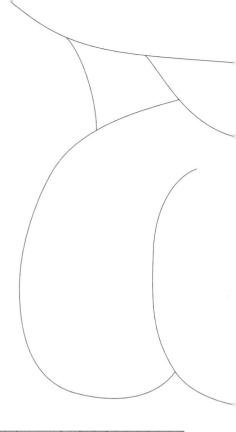

VISUALROUTE

address	www.visualroute.com
concept	In January 1998 Datametrics Systems Corporation launched a piece of software called VisualRoute. Developed in Java, VisualRoute is a trace route program which provides a graphical interpretation of internet networks. The real purpose of this software is to analyse problems with internet connections, for example failure to connect to a certain site. The user simply types in a URL and a graphic of all its network connections appears on a map of the world. The software provides a fast and fascinating look at what goes on behind the pages we see.
credits	Creator of the VisualRoute concept: Jerry Jongerius
software	Written in Java using Microsoft Visual J++

Hop	Err	IP Address	Node Na	Location	ms	Graph	Network
1		204.49.53.4	rocket.gn	Destin, FL 32541	119		Sprint/Centel
2		204.49.53.1	gateway.	Destin, FL 32541	110		Sprint/Centel
3		204.49.13.17	ans-gulfr	Tallahassee, FL 3	146		Sprint/Centel
4	99	204.49.7.17	cisco12-t	Tallahassee, FL 3	147		Sprint/Centel
5		199.44.9.35	cisco8-f5	Tallahassee, FL 3	189		Sprint/Centel
6		144.228.134.9	sl-gw10-l	Fort Worth, TX, US/	166		Sprint
7		208.12.128.2		Herndon, VA 2207	200		Sprint
8		144.232.1.137	sl-bb6-fw	Fort Worth, TX, US	245		Sprint/United Information Service
9	2	144.232.8.158	sl-bb10-p	Pennsauken, NJ, (	201		Sprint/United Information Service
10	1	144.232.5.2		Herndon, VA 2207	215		Sprint/United Information Service
11		144.232.5.86		Herndon, VA 2207	232		Sprint/United Information Service
12	3	192.157.69.65	sprint-na	Pennsauken, NJ, l	231		Sprint NAP Team
13	1	202.232.0.253	Manhatta	New York, NY, US/	220		IIJ Internet
14	3	202.232.0.249	iijgate1.i	-	401		IIJ Internet
15	1	202.232.1.193	osaka-bt	Osaka, Japan	391		IIJ Internet
16	1	202.232.0.54	nagoya-b	Nagoya, Japan	397		IIJ Internet
17	5	202.232.1.226	nagoya0.	Nagoya, Japan	418		IIJ Internet
18	1	202.232.12.18	tnsgw.iij.i	-	439		IIJ Internet
19	1	210.148.240.126		Tokyo 101-0054	421		IIJ Internet
20	1	210.128.150.23	tidweb.to	Tokyo 101-0054	411		IIJ Internet

Hop	Err	IP Address	Node Na	Location	ms	Graph	Network
1		204.49.53.4	rocket.gn	Destin, FL 32541	133		Sprint/Centel
2		204.49.53.1	gateway.	Destin, FL 32541	122		Sprint/Centel
3		204.49.13.17	ans-gulfr	Tallahassee, FL 3	146		Sprint/Centel
4		204.49.7.9	cisco12-t	Tallahassee, FL 3	146		Sprint/Centel
5		199.44.9.35	cisco8-f5	Tallahassee, FL 3	165		Sprint/Centel
6		144.228.134.9	sl-gw10-l	Fort Worth, TX, US.	199		Sprint
7		208.12.128.1	sl-fw-1-Fl	Fort Worth, TX, US.	197		Sprint
8		144.232.1.130	sl-bb4-fw	Fort Worth, TX, US.	351		Sprint/United Information Service
9		144.232.8.54	sl-bb3-se	Seattle, WA, USA	245		Sprint/United Information Service
10		144.232.0.102	sl-bb4-se	Seattle, WA, USA	228		Sprint/United Information Service
11		166.48.18.1	borderco	San Fransisco, CA	419		MCI Internet Services
12		166.48.18.1	borderco	San Fransisco, CA	381		MCI Internet Services
13		166.48.19.250	telstra.Sa	San Fransisco, CA	510		MCI Internet Services
14		139.130.249.229	Fddi0-0.p	Sydney, Australia	514		Australian Academic and Resear
15		139.130.32.26	Serial0-1	Auckland, New Ze.	601		Australian Academic and Resear
16		203.98.4.206	Serial0.r	Wellington, New Z	640		Connectivity Service Provider
17		203.98.4.210			646		Connectivity Service Provider
18		203.97.132.190	wn1-coz.		645		NetLink: Wellington Server hostin
19	1	202.20.93.29	wn9.netli		647		NetLink: NetLink Wellington DMZ
20		203.97.176.34	dia-wn9p		653		NetLink: Wellington Leased line
21		202.49.208.111	network.c	Parliamentary and	696		Additional Class-C nets to suppo
22		202.27.68.60	www.gov	Wellington	694		Government Within Reach

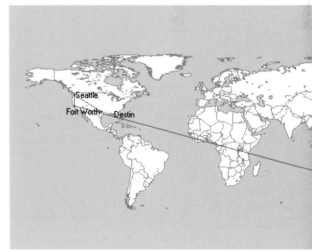

What are your recommended websites?

www.dejanews.com
www.altavista.com
www.yahoo.com
//abcnews.go.com
www.idyll-by-the-sea.com

What single thing would most improve the web from a creative/design point of view?

High-speed internet connections for everyone. Without bandwidth concerns, anything can be created either directly by using HTML or by downloadable code, like Java.

What is the future of the website in terms of design?

Keeping up with new technologies as they emerge.

What will be the next big design trend in websites?

Making websites easier to understand for people, like my parents, who know nothing about computers.

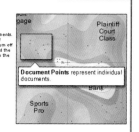

Welcome to the ThemeScape Quick Tour

A ThemeScape is a visual landscape of the information in hundreds - or thousands - of documents and web pages. At a glance you can see the important topics and how they are related.

ThemeScape creates maps by first reading a collection of documents, and then organizing them onto an information landscape based on their content.

QuickTour Subjects
Reading a Map
Browsing Documents
Searching for Documents
Flagging & Sharing Documents

Reading a Map (4 of 7)

Document Points
Document Points represent individual documents. There are typically hundreds or thousands of documents in a map. You can temporarily turn off the document points to make it easier to read the labels by clicking on the document button in the button bar.

Next: Reading a Map - Query Results

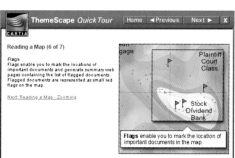

Document Points represent individual documents.

ThemeScape *Quick Tour*   Home   ◄ Previous   Next ►   X

Reading a Map (1 of 7)

A ThemeScape map looks like a topographical map of mountains and valleys. The concept of the layout is simple: documents with similar content are placed closer together, and peaks appear where there is a concentration of closely related documents.

Next: Reading a Map - Peaks

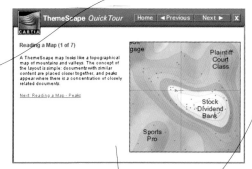

ThemeScape *Quick Tour*   Home   ◄ Previous   Next ►   X

Reading a Map (5 of 7)

Query Results
Query results are drawn as blue points whenever you perform a search or select topics from the topic list. By looking at where the blue dots are drawn on the map, you can immediately see the context in which the results occur.

Next: Reading a Map - Flags

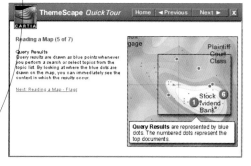

Query Results are represented by blue dots. The numbered dots represent the top documents.

ThemeScape *Quick Tour*   Home   ◄ Previous   Next ►   X

Reading a Map (2 of 7)

Peaks
Peaks represent concentrations of documents about a similar topic. Higher numbers of documents create higher peaks. The valleys between peaks can be interesting because they contain fewer documents and more unique content.

Next: Reading a Map - Topic Labels

Peaks represent concentrations of documents about a similar topic.

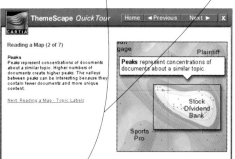

ThemeScape *Quick Tour*   Home   ◄ Previous   Next ►   X

Reading a Map (6 of 7)

Flags
Flags enable you to mark the locations of important documents and generate summary web pages containing the list of flagged documents. Flagged documents are represented as small red flags on the map.

Next: Reading a Map - Zooming

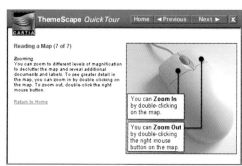

Flags enable you to mark the location of important documents in the map.

ThemeScape *Quick Tour*   Home   ◄ Previous   Next ►   X

Reading a Map (3 of 7)

Topic Labels
Topic Labels reflect the major two or three topics represented in a given area of the map, providing a quick indication of what the documents are about. Additional labels often appear when you zoom into the map for greater detail.

Next: Reading a Map - Document Points

Topic Labels reflect the major topics represented in a given area of the map.

ThemeScape *Quick Tour*   Home   ◄ Previous   Next ►   X

Reading a Map (7 of 7)

Zooming
You can zoom to different levels of magnification to declutter the map and reveal additional documents and labels. To see greater detail in the map, you can zoom in by double clicking on the map. To zoom out, double-click the right mouse button.

Return to Home

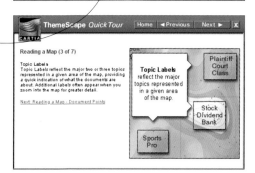

You can **Zoom In** by double-clicking on the map.

You can **Zoom Out** by double-clicking the right mouse button on the map.

THEMESCAPE

address   www.cartia.com

concept   Cartia's ThemeScape software (see introduction) breaks sentences down into constituent parts and looks for common themes. By doing this it begins to understand concepts which are then placed within a multidimensional database. Documents are located according to content and the whole thing is mapped out as a relief map of an island. Hills represent areas where there are lots of documents which share similar concepts. Click on an area and you can drill down into ever greater levels of detail. Shown here is a map of a day's news from the US which has been processed by ThemeScape. More maps like this one are available at www.newsmaps.com.

credits   Software created by Cartia

software   ThemeScape

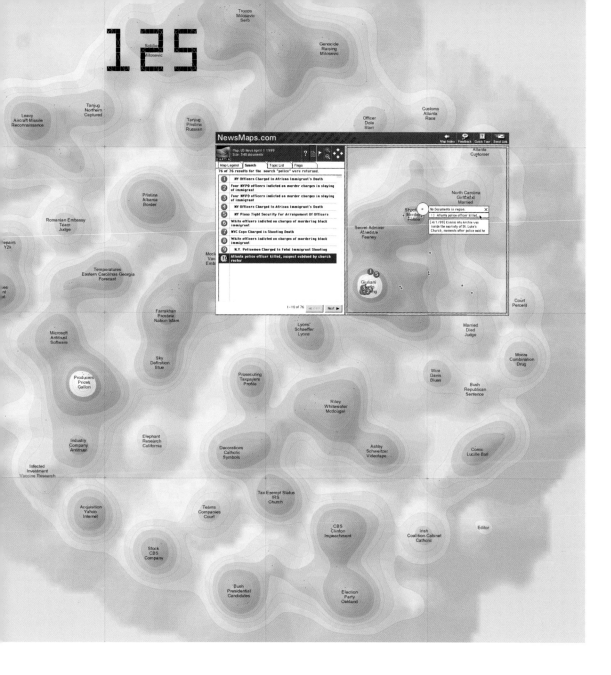

126

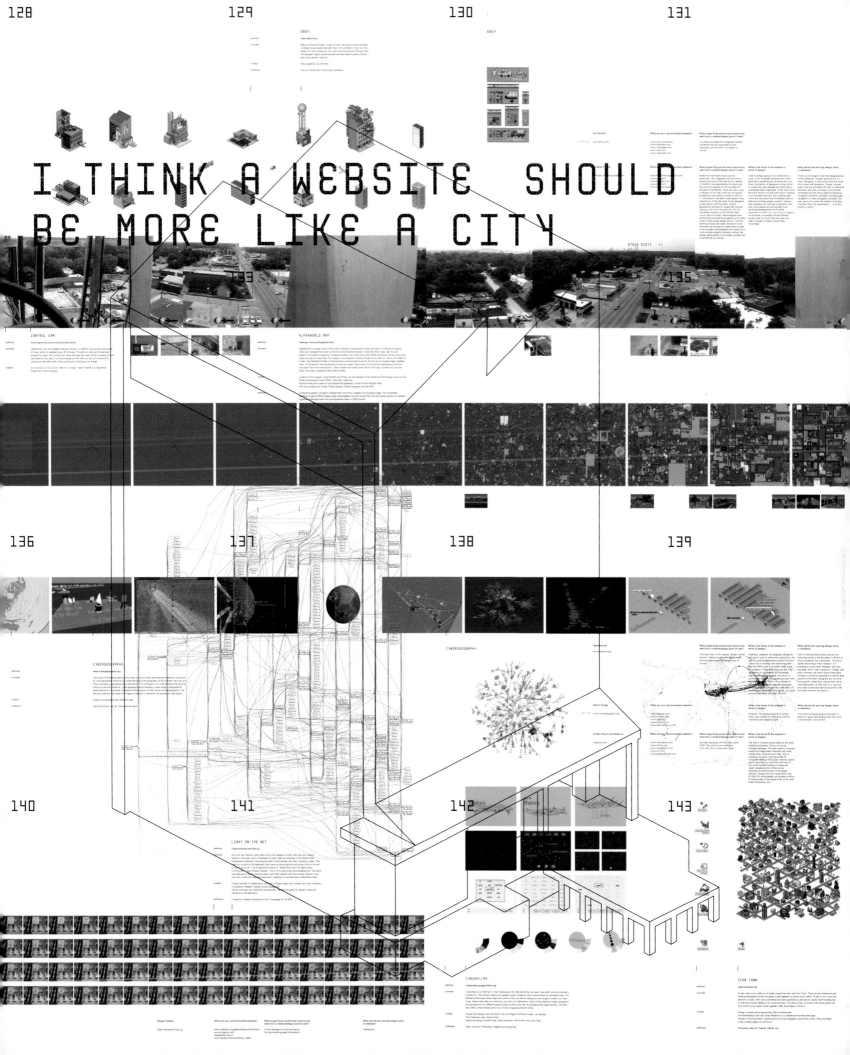

I THINK A WEBSITE SHOULD BE MORE LIKE A CITY

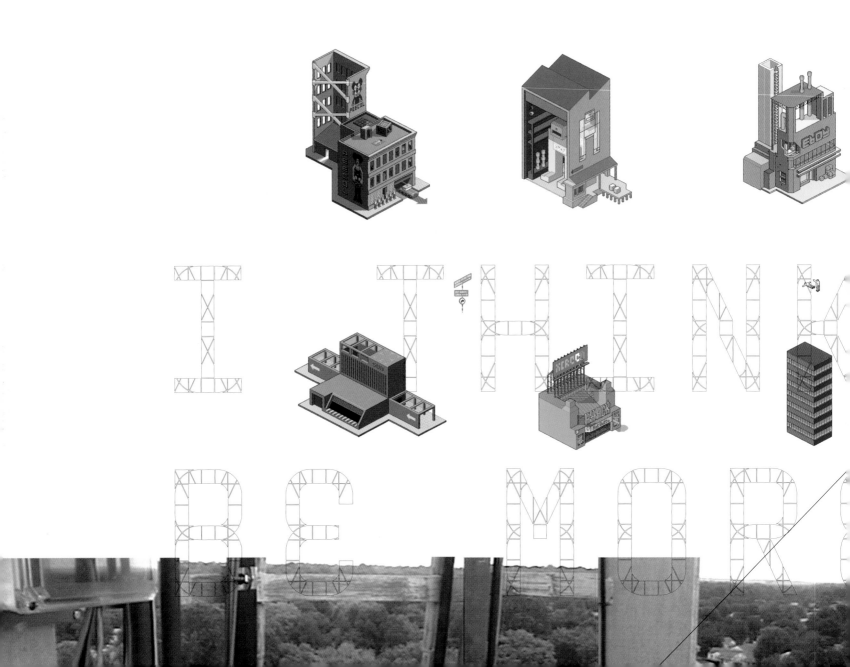

EBOY

address	www.eboy.com
concept	eBoy's aims are simple: 'to get hot jobs, fame and money and girls'. A design group based between New York and Berlin, they not only design for new media, but they sell fonts and pixel art through their homepages. Highly recommended are their Peecol series of fonts and icons, perfect pixel art.
credits	eBoy graphics: Kai Vermehr
software	GoLive Cyberstudio, Photoshop, GifMation

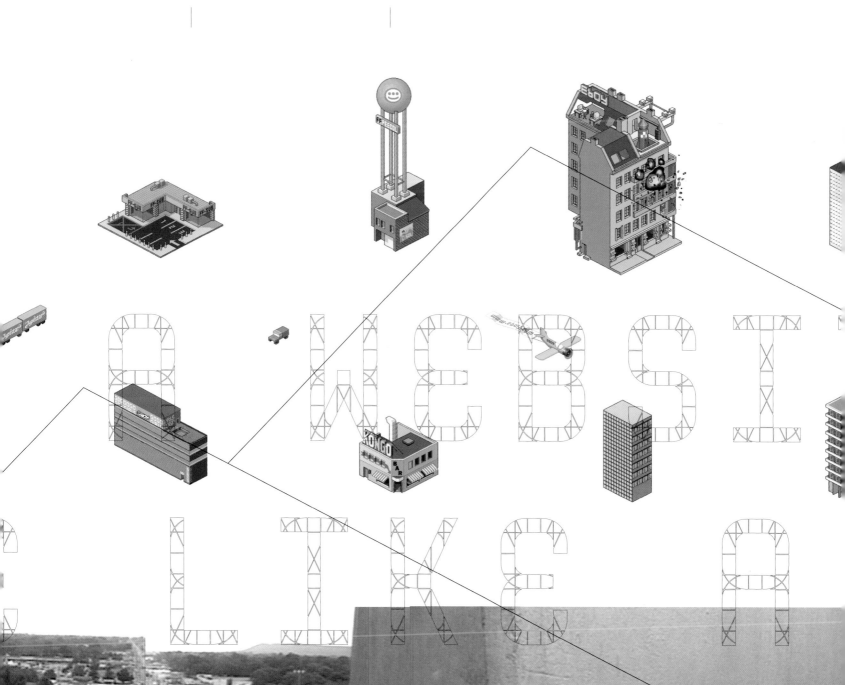

EBOY

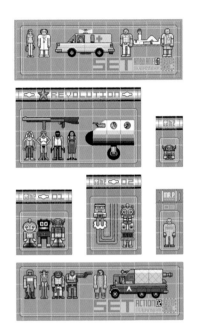

Kai Vermehr

← 128-129   www.eboy.com

Christian Cooper

Principal, megacorp.graphikom

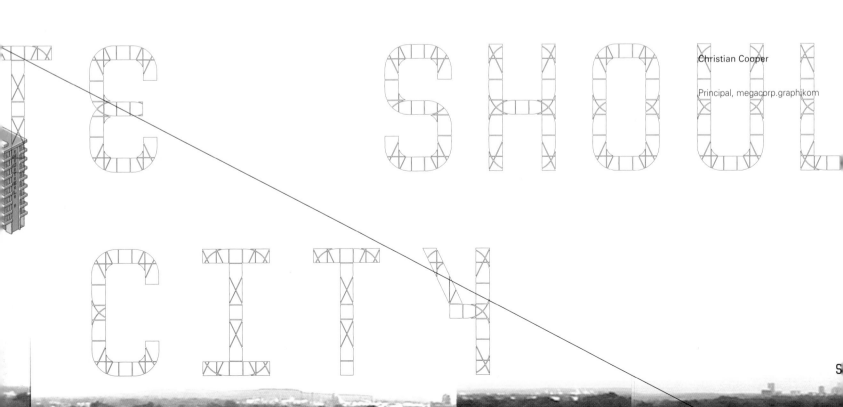

What are your recommended websites?

www.acne.se/netbaby
www.kraftwerk.com
www.hotwheels.com
www.cnet.com
www.macsurfer.com

What single thing would most improve the web from a creative/design point of view?

A simple and stable font-integration system. Standards that are supported by both Netscape and Microsoft. And speed of course.

What are your recommended websites?

www.theschwacorporation.com
www.nike.com
www.budpeen.com
www.blind.com
www.klaskey-csupo.com

What single thing would most improve the web from a creative/design point of view?

Aside from technical issues such as bandwidth, net congestion and the bulk of people browsing worldwide at slow speeds (14.4/28.8), the responsibility for improving the web sits squarely on the shoulders of designers themselves. There are many ways to design for the web which do not require prospective site visitors to have an ISDN or t-1 connection to be able to participate in the interactivity of the site itself. Some designers simply author with the latest, hottest applications and tend to forget that they are utilizing a new form of public art. Like the proverbial museum on the hill that many cannot afford to enter, these designers are locking the overwhelming majority out of sites which contain great design and art. Until the technical issues are totally resolved so that everyone can browse at a speed fast enough to be included, and designers can utilize much more complex graphic solutions without the design taking aeons to download, perhaps this is something to consider.

What is the future of the website in terms of design?

I see it perhaps going in two directions at once, a sort of parallel development which becomes a perpendicular development over time. One faction of designers will go full-tilt to create the most detailed and information-overloaded sites imaginable. At the same time the other faction will strip sites down, heading in a minimalist direction, and creating sites which are very direct and immediate without bells-and-whistles graphic overkill. I believe that websites will continue to become more and more interactive with perhaps such revolting developments as an online courtroom in which you may bring suit against an individual, or perhaps remote camera access sites on which one may view live video footage of others without their knowledge.

What will be the next big design trend in websites?

I think we will begin to see the disappearance of the traditional 'margins and buttons' on sites. Navigation is becoming more and more of an issue with designers. Simple 'mouse-overs' and tiny animated GIF files will become obsolete, and sites will begin to be entirely centralized around clever graphic/interactive navigation elements, perhaps including audio navigation or video navigation consoles. We may see a time when the content is far less important than the presentation… or is this already a reality?

CONTROL CAM

address	www.teamtulsa.com/livecams/index.shtml
concept	Oklahoma's only controllable internet camera is a 2NEWS Control-Cam panorama of Tulsa, which is updated every 30 minutes. Though live web cams have been popular for years, the Control-Cam takes the idea one step further by being remote controlled by the user. It is truly amazing to think that you can turn and point a camera on the other side of the world just by clicking on an image.
credits	All materials on this site © 1998 E.W. Scripps. Team Tulsa ® is a registered trademark of the company.

ALPHAWORLD MAP

address   //awmap.vevo.com/toplevel.html

concept   AlphaWorld is a large virtual world with hundreds of thousands of users and tens of millions of objects. Users can navigate the world via the 3D Active Worlds browser, which lets them walk, talk, fly and teleport from place to place as humanoid avatars. But when the world is 655 kilometres across, and when users can see no more than 120 metres in any direction, finding things can be difficult. Hence the need for a map. The AlphaWorld Map is structured as a twelve-level pyramid. At the top is a single-image 'satellite view'; at the bottom are thousands of close-up images. Each level of the pyramid represents a factor-of-two zoom from the level above it, which means the overall zoom factor from top to bottom is just over 2000. The map is updated every three months.

credits   Creation of the mapper: Greg Roelofs and Pieter van der Meulen of the Advanced Technology Group at the Philips Multimedia Center (PMC), Palo Alto, California
Technical help and copies of the AlphaWorld database: Circle of Fire's Roland Vilett
The vevo project as a whole: Philips Design, Philips Research and the PMC

software   A special-purpose C program merged each set of four maplets into a single image. The completed quadtree of gzip'd PPM images were web-enabled via a CGI script that cuts and pastes pieces of maplets together, enhances them and recompresses them in JPEG format

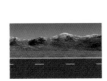

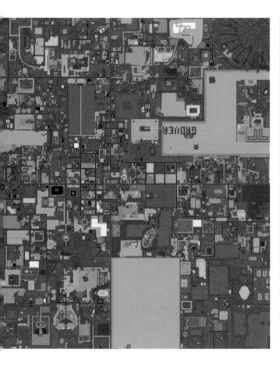 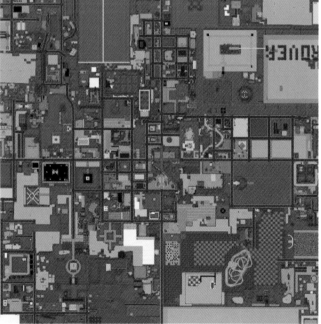 

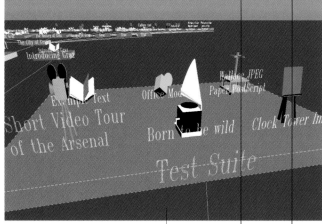

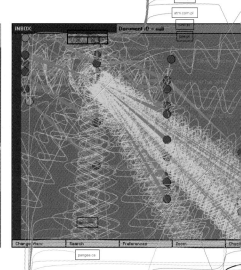

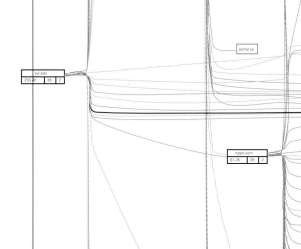

CYBERGEOGRAPHY

address

www.cybergeography.org

concept

The study of emerging cyber-communities is now an exact and important science. Sites such as cyber-geography enhance our understanding of the geography of the internet, the web and other emerging cyberspaces and cyberplaces. The emphasis is on understanding the physical infrastructure and statistics. Cyber-geography encompasses a wide range of geographical phenomena from the study of physical infrastructure to traffic flows and demographics. The site also explores the maps and images employed to represent the spaces of cyberspace.

credits

Design and programming: Martin Dodge

software

Microsoft Word, ws_ftp, Netscape Navigator

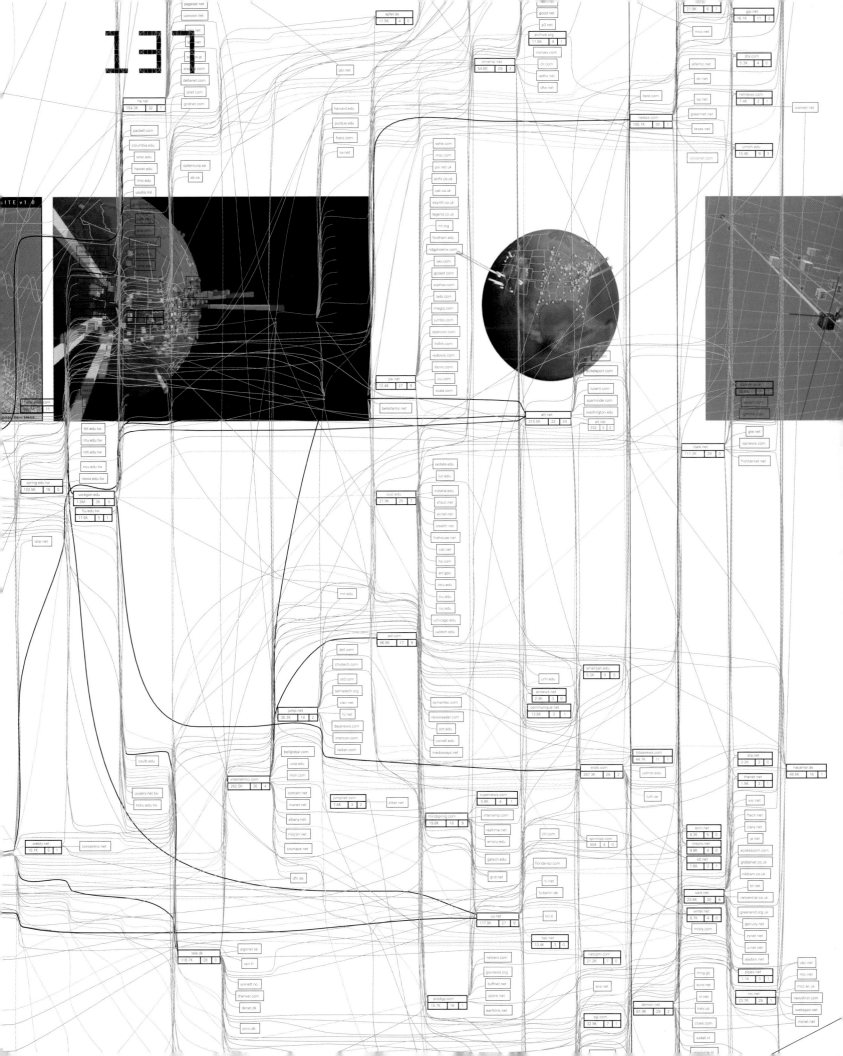

137

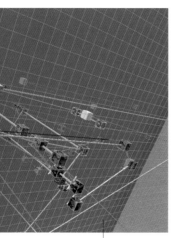 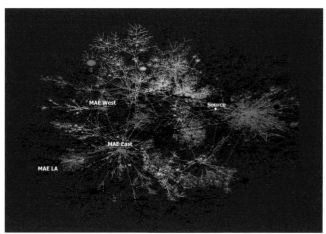 

CYBERGEOGRAPHY

Geert Lovink

www.nettime.org

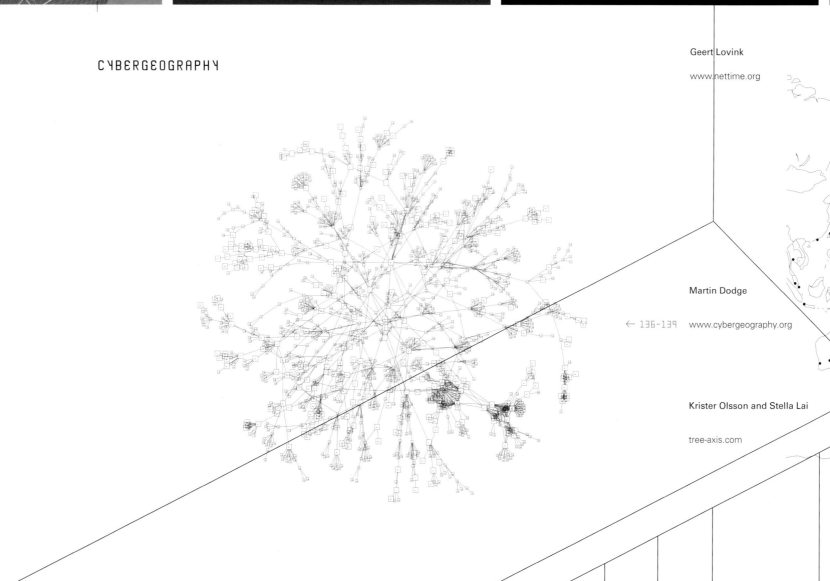

Martin Dodge

← 136-139 www.cybergeography.org

Krister Olsson and Stella Lai

tree-axis.com

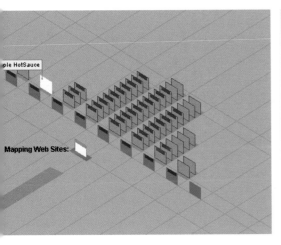

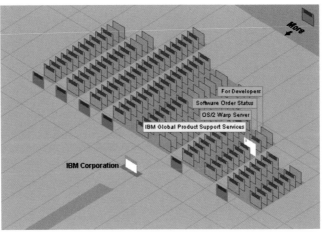

What single thing would most improve the web from a creative/design point of view?

Software rules, in this respect; design comes second. I believe in software determinism. And ultimately hardware dictatorship, of course.

What are your recommended websites?

www.altavista.com
www.amazon.com
www.caida.org
www.yahoo.co.uk
www.datametrics.com:81

What are your recommended websites?

www.volumeone.com
www.shift.jp.org
www.typographic.com
www.e13.com
www.antennadesign.com

What single thing would most improve the web from a creative/design point of view?

Browser standards. DHTML that works. DOM. The usual buzzwords! And a G3 with DSL on everyone's desk.

What is the future of the website in terms of design?

Hopefully, websites will disappear altogether, and 'grow' back to where they came from, the text-only archive and communication function. I know this is nostalgic and reactionary, but I fear the VRML type of so-called visual ways of navigation. That's pure horror for me. I do not believe in visualization of knowledge. That is backwardness to me, the return of iconoclastic rule. We should always overcome the rule of images. What is now needed is the democratization of computer languages, the spreading of software into wide areas of society and indeed the entire planet, not some baroque interfaces and élitist 3D-isms.

What is the future of the website in terms of design?

Evolution. The gradual growth of content. More user interactivity. Real-time internet monitoring and mapping tools.

What is the future of the website in terms of design?

The web is currently being hailed as the great publishing equalizer. This is, of course, complete garbage. The vast majority of people publishing independent websites are white, middle-class, American and male. This is changing, however, with the prices of computers falling, more public internet access points sprouting up, and more and more of the world (outside America, Europe and Japan) developing the infrastructure necessary to become part of the global network. People who buy inexpensive (sub-$1,000) PCs will probably not be able to afford or have access to the typical tools of the web trade (Photoshop, etc.).

What will be the next big design trend in websites?

Who is making these trends, and are we following trends in the first place? I think it is time to question this mechanism. The net is rapidly becoming a mass medium, it is reaching a critical mass. Mergers, sell outs, big deals, that's what is going on. Design, and even software, are minor topics these days. Perhaps it is time for designers to rethink their position in the field. Designers are now at a turning point: either they reduce their role to mere decoration, or they look for a way out and make a historical deal/compromise with the (free) software developers.

What will be the next big design trend in websites?

The end of annoying plug-ins and back to basics for good, fast-loading sites that work in all browsers, not just IE4.

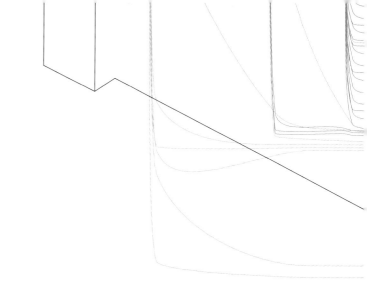

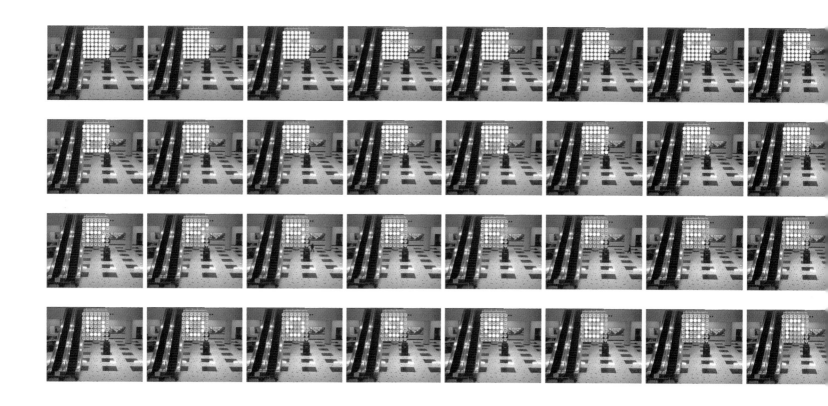

Masaki Fujihata

↗ //light.softopia.pref.gifu.jp

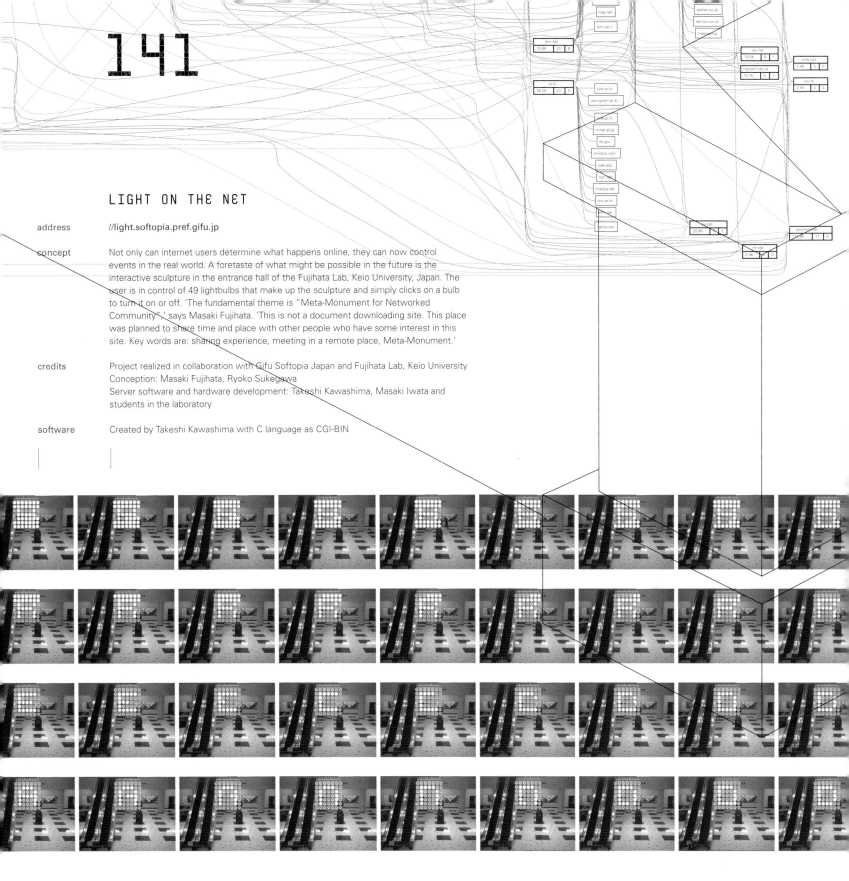

LIGHT ON THE NET

address	//light.softopia.pref.gifu.jp
concept	Not only can internet users determine what happens online, they can now control events in the real world. A foretaste of what might be possible in the future is the interactive sculpture in the entrance hall of the Fujihata Lab, Keio University, Japan. The user is in control of 49 lightbulbs that make up the sculpture and simply clicks on a bulb to turn it on or off. 'The fundamental theme is "Meta-Monument for Networked Community",' says Masaki Fujihata. 'This is not a document downloading site. This place was planned to share time and place with other people who have some interest in this site. Key words are: sharing experience, meeting in a remote place, Meta-Monument.'
credits	Project realized in collaboration with Gifu Softopia Japan and Fujihata Lab, Keio University Conception: Masaki Fujihata, Ryoko Sukegawa Server software and hardware development: Takeshi Kawashima, Masaki Iwata and students in the laboratory
software	Created by Takeshi Kawashima with C language as CGI-BIN

What are your recommended websites?

www.walkerart.org/gallery9/beyondinterface
www.longnow.com
//telegarden.aec.at
www.oanda.com/converter/cc_table

What single thing would most improve the web from a creative/design point of view?

A new paradigm of communication.
Not downloading paper documents.

What will be the next big design trend in websites?

Interactivity.

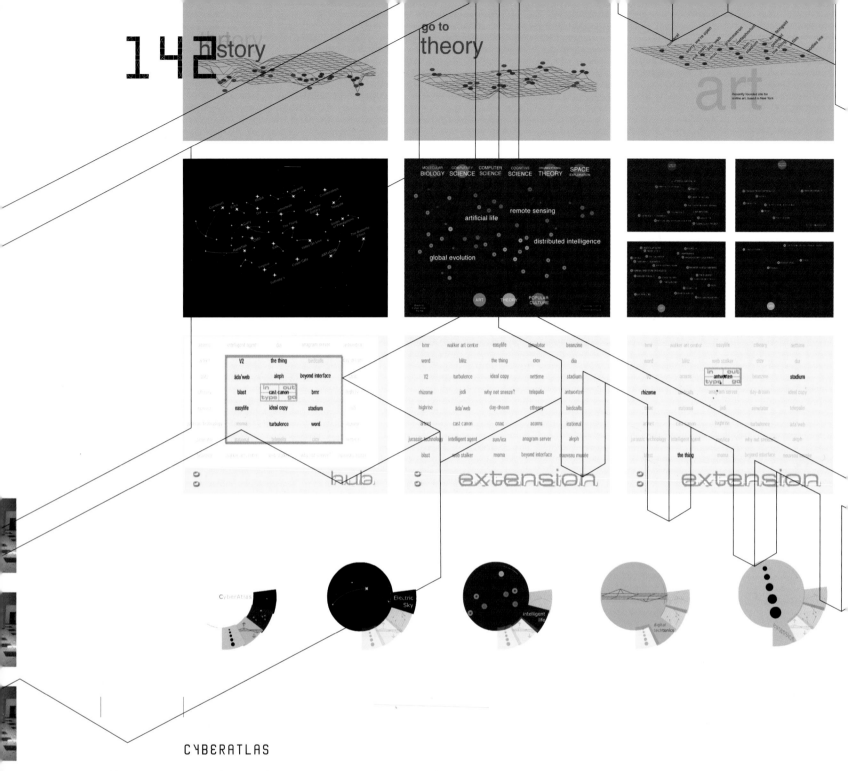

CYBERATLAS

address	//cyberatlas.guggenheim.org
concept	CyberAtlas is an attempt to chart cyberspace, the idea being that net users 'feel adrift without landmarks to steer by'. The various maps act as graphic search engines with a concentration on art-based sites. The difference between these maps and others is that, as well as telling you how to get to where you want to go, these maps take you there too: just click on a destination. Each of the interactive maps represents the perspective of a different guest curator or artist who has reconnoitered the digital domain. The site also offers critical essays and a tour of other mapping projects online.
credits	Overall site design, plus the Electric Sky and Digital Techtonics maps: Jon Ippolito The Extension map: Ainatte Inbal Additional design: Ainatte Inbal, Debra Hampton, Mia Hurley and Laura Trippi
software	Flash, Director, Photoshop, Pagemill and JavaScript